P9-ELX-256

Taste of Tears•Touch of God

Taste of Tears
Touch of God

Ann Kiemel Anderson

A Division of Thomas Nelson Publishers
Nashville • Atlanta • Camden • New York

Copyright © 1984 by Ann Kiemel Anderson

All rights reserved. Written permission must be secured from the publisher to use or reproduce any part of this book, except for brief quotations in critical reviews or articles.

Published in Nashville, Tennessee by Oliver-Nelson Books, a division of Thomas Nelson, Inc. and distributed in Canada by Lawson Falle, Ltd., Cambridge, Ontario.

Printed in the United States of America.

Fourth printing

Library of Congress Cataloging in Publication Data

Anderson, Ann Kiemel.
  Taste of tears, touch of God.

  1. Anderson, Ann Kiemel. 2. Wives—United States—Biography. 3. Wives—United States—Religious life. 4. Infertility—Religious aspects—Christianity.
I. Title
HQ759.A475 1984   306.8'1'0924   84-1139
ISBN 0-8407-9025-2

Acknowledgments

Page 16, "God Leads Us Along," G.A. Young, Lillenas Publishing Co., Kansas City, Mo.; pages 39 and 50, "Faith," Ella Wheeler Wilcox, W.B. Conkey Co., Hammond, Ind.; page 94, "Let The Son of God Enfold You," John Wimber, Maranatha Music, Costa Mesa, Cal.; page 110, "In His Time," Diane Ball, "Praise Four," Maranatha Music, Word Books, Waco, Tx.; page 163, "The Velveteen Rabbit," Margery Williams, Doubleday, New York, N.Y.; page 197, "Hast Thou No Scar," Amy Carmichael, Christian Literature Crusade, Inc., Fort Washington, Pa.; page 192, "I Will Sing to My Child," Merilee Zdenek, "Someone Special," Word Books, Waco, Tx.

to pam

secretary. comrade. dreamer.
child of holiness preacher, as i.
singer of all the old hymns.
every verse.
beside me, to taste my tears.

and clyde

crippled with arthritis. fellow sufferer.
cared for by his loving, ninety–year–old
mother, anna. brave. generous. will's
and my dear friend.

"…in God's own time and way
i will know again your smile some glad and happy
day
when we have met a strong young man and called
him 'God'
and watched Him flash a rainbow from a golden
rod.

to gently brush EARTH'S tears from off our face
and leave but shining joy to take their place…"

c.w.

contents

i know the taste of tears   15
a love for babies   23
my turn to have a baby   26
no running for twelve days   32
infertility, a real problem   35
disappointment again   38
a round-the-world trip   46
my exciting husband   51
an exquisite outfit   58
on a roller coaster   62
new hope   68
conception   71
emergency   74
miscarriage   80
meanwhile, in dallas...   83
the hope chest   86
a deeper "yes" than ever before   89
another emergency   93
trusting God is not always easy   96
would we want to adopt   100
marital agreement is not always easy   104
questioning will, questioning God   107
once again, the divine call   115
a new way of "seeing"   118
will hears my first speech   124
my struggle with will's books   127
the ranch   130
the blessing that maketh rich   138
sundays, our toughest days   142
a time for reflection   145
first love   149
a new opportunity   165
our first vacation together   170
another baby needs a home   182
decision time   185
hope turns to disappointment   195
a final word to you, my friends   198
God's special surprise   201

foreword

Thirty-eight years ago, after nine months in a womb together, Ann and I were born into this world. Ann was born first, leading the way for my entrance, and this leadership role is one she has played through most of our life together. From my earliest recollections I recall Ann as several steps ahead of me. She always seemed to know more and have a greater grasp on what was the best direction to take. She talked for me, directed me, led me, took care of me, and became the person I most trusted in life. I grew up believing she really had some Godlike power that could protect me and help me make it through any obstacle of life. It seemed she always did better in school. It was she who would think to write a special poem or create a picture for one of us in the family and present it at the dinner table. When we were in junior high school she entered a contest for both of us in which she wrote a letter to the governor's wife about why our mother was so special. The writers of the winning letters were invited with their mothers to the governor's mansion for tea. Her letter was one of those accepted.

I early developed a feeling of apprehension about what clever, winning idea she would come up with next because, while I got to share in some of the glory, more often I was left standing on the sidelines feeling inadequate and inferior. I found myself entering speech contests just to keep her from getting too far "ahead" of me, and in fear of pitiful glances I would collect from people comparing us.

I grew up honestly not knowing who I was because most of me seemed somehow strangely to be connected to who *she* was—that is, the "good," "worthwhile" part of me. The rest of me felt too insignificant and worthless to notice. Ann ended college in glory and seemed to continue to climb to heights beyond even her greatest expectations.

I've spent most of my life—while she achieved, gained applause, took on a job, and transformed something "ordinary into something spectacular"—smiling on the outside, giving the appearance of not noticing my "vanilla" state, and then racing to a bathroom or to my pillow and sobbing with an overwhelming sense of pain and agony over my total insignificance.

I did lead the way into marriage, which was most courageous for someone who had never led before.

When Ann began writing books and speaking across the country, I stumbled to graduate school, desperately looking for some way to "hold my own." I graduated with a master's degree in clinical therapy and began a private practice in marriage, family, and individual counseling. I then led the way into motherhood, which was even more terrifying than marriage. Tom and I both agreed, as we looked at both sides of our families, that we could either produce something wonderful or an absolute freak. Watching my body balloon out of proportion only increased my terror of what was growing inside. Tom and I did, however, produce a beautiful, perfect son; and two and a half years later, a second one.

When Ann married Will Anderson two years ago, I finally reached an end of my agony of inferiority. Not only did I always feel inferior to Ann, but we also grew up in a culture in which Ann and I both suffered from being "haolies," outsiders, and blatantly "inferior" again. I vowed at her wedding that, whatever it took, God and I would climb beyond any pain and someday, even if it took *forever*, I would find a place equal to Ann's. My goal was not to measure up to her achievement, but rather internally to come to peace with myself so that her accomplishments no longer threatened me. In a quiet way, I began to detach and find myself.

It is at this point in Ann's life that this book begins,

for when Ann married and moved across the country, she began the greatest personal journey of her life. For the first time in our relationship she began to reach out, and at moments even cling to me for help, words of hope and encouragement. The adjustment of marriage (I don't think anyone has yet captured on paper the full picture of marriage!) and the inability to achieve the only thing in her life she had set out to do— that is, to bear a child, brought her deep and close to her truest, most authentic "self." This was a self she had learned very early in life to cover up, to compensate for. I began to hear her talk about and experience the kind of pain I had struggled with for most of my life.

In the last two years we have come closer together than we have been since the earliest days of our existence. We are more alike than I would ever have guessed. At the deepest level of who we are is this raging fear of failure and fear of returning to the sense of total insignificance I realize we both felt as children.

While I have never had trouble conceiving and bearing a child, the story on these pages is really more than Ann's story—it is *our* story. It is the story of the struggles of twinhood, our growing up in a culture that rejected us, our lifelong search for what wholeness really is, and our wondering where and who God is at moments of confusion. While the details of our journeys are unique, it is also the story of many with whom I have worked professionally and many who will read the book.

I have walked many hours with Ann these last two years and I have seen her struggle and fight and never give up, and I have to admit she is still my "hero." She is an amazing woman with a magnanimous love like Mary in the New Testament, who poured costly perfume on the feet of Jesus. I have never seen anyone love and care and give so extravagantly to people around her as Ann.

Through our deep pain and pursuit of self-worth we have both discovered more clearly than ever before that being touched by Jesus is the greatest hope and answer for any human life. My prayer is that as you read this book, you too will receive a new touch from Jesus!

Jan Kiemel Ream
February 1984

i know
the
taste
of
tears

i hid them often in my throat or wrapped in pillow-cases where no one would find them. i felt ugly, and all the pretty clothes and a husband telling me every day i was beautiful could not change a feeling that only i, with God, could resolve. most of all, i began to hate my body because it would not do what i wanted it to. it was always catching infections. turning out negative pregnancy tests. every month, defeat and tears.

i was left with nothing but the ugly little seed of what i REALLY felt about myself. God taking all the sham and knocking down every single fake stone of foundation. God trying me through fire to rebuild my structure. to start back at the beginning. to make me truly whole. to make me holy.

"some through the water…some through the flood…some through the fire…but all through the Blood…some through great sorrow…BUT God gives a song…."

i struggled to hear the song.

it kept getting lost. black shadows and ominous darkness washed it away again and again. sometimes i tasted death. and sometimes it seemed sweet compared to life. to hopelessness.

i have tasted more tears in two years than all the thirty-five before them. i have walked through the fire. the edges of my heels…my soul…singed. i have found quiet places, far from anyone's ears, and screamed out the pain. let it run out my eyes and nose…releasing the pressure. keeping the explosion away. will, my husband, has held me tightly in his arms on dark, late, lonely nights, and let my tears bathe his face and shoulder, his warm skin caressing my sorrow.

but God HAS touched me. has given me what no other gift but pain can bestow. has pulled me back to Himself, and away from self-love that comes from the great fear of rejection.

I carefully lay my story before you. different, yes, very different, from all the other stories of mine you might have read.

i lived in a pretty house. a new bride to a very
strong, handsome, no–nonsense, exciting man.
dark, flashing eyes. straight back. broad shoulders.
wiry, black, thick curly hair. a thinker. an idea
man. a doer. a risker. the unexpected his terrain.
often, will would pick me up in the kitchen and
with laughter carry me off to bed. or we would
drive to jackson hole or sun valley for a weekend
of skiing and ice–cream cones and roaring fires in
cozy, lovely places. sometimes after flying in from
a speaking trip, i would find a beautiful black
negligee or other special gift wrapped on my
pillow. this man who says he never needed anyone
in his life...until me. rugged. straightforward.
fearless. yet somewhere deep inside him, i have
found a gentle place. a soft, tender spot.

it is very difficult, with all of these good things, to
write about my tears. to be more vulnerable on
paper than ever before. though i did not expect it,
all the transition and change resulting from
marriage and moving from boston to idaho carried
my sense of security away. i was as terrified and
helpless and lost as if i had become paralyzed or
blind.

gradually, i began to discover this great, inferior
place in me. hidden all these years. on reflection, it
seems to me, at sometime, when i was small...it
must have been when my family lived in
hawaii...i came to believe i was a defective person.
not defective in my thinking or my learning or my

17

walk with God, but in my body. to be SO white in a sea of such brown skins. i did not come from an athletic family, so i never excelled in individualized sports, which i think gives one great self-confidence. years ago, our church was very strict on lipstick and makeup, which made jan, my sister, and me feel all the more estranged.

as a child, outside my family unit, i felt i was nothing. of absolutely no value or admiration to ANYONE. but some deep, fierce, unknown spirit inside me decided to change that…to become so nice, so creative, so loving, so smart, so good that the world would love me. notice me. appreciate me. value me.

it was not until i married…moved to idaho…that this facade began to crumble and the reality of all of this began to unfold for me.

overnight, i moved away from all my productivity and structure and security and identity. away from singleness and control of my own life to being married and under the authority of a very strong man. stopped. suddenly. far away. knowing will only six months before we married. i have NEVER questioned that decision. but will had been independent for thirty-eight years. was not an "intimate" person. was struggling to keep his own sense of structure and order and discipline when now there were two to concern himself with.

all the years of covering my deep inferiority. my
unhealthy, shaking fear that i might feel the awful
pain of rejection again. that i might become a
nonperson like i felt as a child. this fear and
uncertainty loomed larger all the time. living in
this small community, all that really seemed to
matter was having babies, and i could not, no
matter how fiercely i tried, make even that happen
in my body.

giving up running to help in my pregnancy
struggle. still no babies. trying to think of what to
say to women whose worlds were diaper bags and
nursing and gardening and canning vegetables.

fearfully, i felt people in this small idaho
community expected me, will anderson's new
bride, to fly in and share God's love with
everyone. i was suddenly very shy. i faced a
neighborhood instead of a downtown
condominium building. talk of potatoes and alfalfa
and huge farm machinery and cattle, instead of
quiet restaurants with white tablecloths and men
in double-breasted suits.

i did find lots of children to love there. will and i
have bought many ice-cream cones. one sunday,
we piled all the preschoolers from our church into
our car. scrunched in. standing. on our laps. will
opened the sun roof, and some sort of breathed out
it. it was during church. we headed to
baskin-robbins. bought all of them what they

wanted. sang sunday school songs to the girls
behind the counter. will and i ran from one child to
the next to try to catch enormous globs of ice
cream dripping down sunday dresses and shirts.

i have taken little girls shopping, and brought
surprises back to children from my speaking trips.
but i missed my boston "ghetto" children. the
narrow streets. the old buildings. mothers
screaming out of windows. small, fragile boys and
girls who really seemed to NEED me.

even with jan, my twin sister. my closest person in
the world. my womb–sharer. my childhood
secret-teller. even with jan, i began to feel lost. all
our lives, i had been the leader. for years i had
dragged jan after me, chasing great dreams and
new missions and God's ideas. i was so brave and
assured, always pulling her along, trying to make
her feel as i did. and now, while i was backing
away from a professional career and staying home
much more and trying to become more
"everyday," she was building a thriving therapy
clinic. was being asked to speak everywhere as a
psychologist, and rightly so. she IS TERRIFIC!
suddenly, i was the follower. looking on in
admiration, but overwhelmed with nothingness
standing next to her.

and she had two beautiful, healthy sons, whereas i
could not produce even one.

trying to be a good wife, a creative cook, a faithful housekeeper still left me with hours of unfilled time. jan was changing all the wounded and broken lives in her office. raising children. working on a business with tom. she was shaking the world, and i could not find even a small mission in a quiet community.

but let's begin at the beginning....

a love for babies

dolls were my favorite thing. jan and i played with
them for hours. we picked couples in the church
that we thought were exciting, and pretended we
were they. taking on their names. talking to our
"husbands." scolding our children. pretending we
were pregnant. walking with our eight-year-old
backs curved in to protrude our stomachs as much
as possible. i would get out of bed at night and
make sure my dolls were covered, fearful they
might get cold.

every year, my mother's most earnest Christmas
shopping was for new dolls for jan and me. we did
not want decorative dolls or bride dolls or
barbie–type dolls. we wanted BABY dolls. she
would try to find, in the entire city, the
most-like-baby replicas she could. one year, she had
bought us BIG baby dolls, maybe three feet long.
jan came running into the living room Christmas

morning, saw the spectacular dolls, and cried, "oh, my baby!" tears shining in her eyes.

the next Christmas, mother had a man in our church make bunk beds for our BIG dolls. they could be taken apart, making twin beds. she fixed mattresses, fitted sheets...we were overwhelmed, and occupied for years in our play.

my parents' church in hawaii was designed for the islands. open down the sides for the trade winds. at the back was a simple, small nursery, and jan and i spent every service looking and hoping for one of the families with several small children to walk in, so we could go back and keep the nursery during the service.

a time came when jan and i decided to pray for a baby to come to our family. our home needed a baby, we thought. dolls were not good enough.

we dragged to our little bedroom in hawaii an old dresser-drawers. we began asking all the mothers with babies for their old baby clothes. jan and i would take these old clothes and wash them and fold them and organize them in the little drawers. and we prayed...every day...that God would bring a baby to us.

MY MOTHER WAS HORRIFIED!

she was sure God would answer our prayers through her. and she wasn't ready to have another baby. my father had to talk her into having us. she had been happy with one baby.

my parents went to the foster service and begged them for a baby. "i'm sure if our twins have a baby for a few weeks they'll realize that it is not nearly as fun as it may look. if you could only help us…the girls are praying so hard. they have so much faith…we're sure God is going to give US another one."

after a year and a half…praying and believing and filling the chest of drawers…jan and i were handed a little hawaiian baby. newborn. with all the diapers and bottles. we did everything for this baby. prepared her formula. got up in the dark. did all the laundry. we loved this baby. she was ours! but only for a while, of course.

my turn to have a baby

marrying at thirty-five, i wanted a baby my first
year. i had been on my own. tried to share God's
love with the world. now it was MY turn to live
out my childhood fantasies and dreams.

i could do that, to some extent, through jan's
pregnancies and children. i was as awed and full of
wonder through her two pregnancies as she was.
the night tre, her firstborn, arrived i was speaking
in a snow-covered little church in massachusetts. it
took all i had to stand and share, my heart
skipping every other beat. my mind zooming
across my words to cleveland, where i knew jan
was in labor. she had called when she first arrived
in the labor room, to tell me she felt fine. was
relaxed. suspected it would be easy delivering.
knowing nothing about it, of course. she mentioned
women were screaming around her and wished
they had more control. she promised to call me

again, in a while, and let me know how she was, but i never heard back from her.

growing up with such terrible concepts of ourselves, we neither one knew what jan would produce. everyone else had babies, but could that possibly happen to her? would this "person" come out something different? could she REALLY produce a baby, with fingers and toes and a clear little face? we were both almost paralyzed by fear.

after i spoke, before questions and answers, i suggested everyone sing one song and i slipped off the stage to a phone. fingers shaking, i dialed the hospital's number from a little piece of paper wadded in my hand.

"mrs. ream is doing fine. the baby is fine. she is in recovery."

"oh, ma'am, excuse me, but do you know what she had? i am her sister, calling long distance."

"a boy."

"a BOY?!! oh, really a BOY!!"

i started sobbing…stumbled out a "thank you," and hung up. she did it!! she REALLY delivered a baby. i flew back to the stage and announced i was an aunt, for the first time, of a normal, healthy nephew. my eyes were shining. it will be a night i will NEVER forget. january 22, 1976. her husband, tom, did tell me later that soon after our earlier conversation, jan was screaming like the rest of the women in labor. smile.

since we wanted a baby as soon as we could have one, will and i decided not to use contraceptives. we would just let God bring pregnancy about as soon as He desired. little did either of us know what was ahead. we had both, for years, heard of illegitimate children and the horrors of abortion, and we knew NOTHING of infertility. today, it is reported that one in five couples has this problem.

i was still running, though more and more articles were coming out with facts related to long-distance running and conception. i HAD to run. it was the one thing that made me feel the best about myself. and being a bride, with the fresh desire to cook for my big, strong, always-hungry husband, i had been eating more than ever in my life. i weighed eight pounds more than when i had married. running gave me a way to burn off some of the calories. it added structure to my life, something i had always needed for security.

a few months after i married, i became violently ill during my period. we had decided on an obstetrician-gynecologist in pocatello, fifty miles away. on that particular day, he was on vacation. and when i called, sobbing in pain, the answering service transferred me to dr. don dyer, who was handling the other doctor's calls. they told me to come to pocatello immediately. it sounded as if i might even have a tubal pregnancy. will was unavailable, so i just asked my secretary, pam boston, to come and drive me the fifty miles.

all the way over, i was huddled on my side of the car, writhing and crying and hanging onto the dash. i had just thrown my coat on over my flannel nightgown, with knee socks and loafers. it was march 14, 1982.

walking in to see a doctor with whom i had no connection, in a piece of the world that was still very foreign and far away from all the familiar and secure things, in my nightgown, without will, was difficult. tears streaming down my face, barely able to stand up, i was immediately led by the nurse out of the crowded waiting room and into one of the back rooms, where she and dr. dyer focused on me. they were the kindest, gentlest, most professional ones of their profession i had ever encountered, and i was someone they had never even seen before.

very quickly, dr. dyer had me taken to the hospital, given a strong shot for pain, and prepared for an ultrasound. he thought he saw some abnormality, and i was very quickly prepped for surgery. pam was trying to reach will, as i was begging for him, more frightened and alone than i had ever felt before. minutes before they wheeled me to · surgery, will walked into my room. business suit, tie a little loosened at the collar, black eyes flashing

with concern and warmth. he grabbed dr. dyer's
hand (he had been standing beside my bed, waiting
for the orderly) and mine, saying,

"let's say a quick prayer."

he kissed me. promised he would NOT leave. i was
whisked behind "no entry" doors to the cold room
and glaring lights of what i began to know as
"operating rooms."

i remember HOW sick i was when i awakened in
recovery. my skin crawling in reaction to the
anesthesia given to me. violently nauseated,
terrified. what if dr. dyer told me i could never
have any children? it was beyond my ability to
accept at that point. groggily i moved my hand
over my stomach to see if i could find some great
incision where they had removed a tube or all my
female organs, but all i felt was one small patch
and i was comforted.

a nurse informed me i was too sick to go home that
night, and would have to spend the night.
probably no one hates hospitals more than i.
begging and pleading, through tears, did no good,
and i was put in a big, old room, with my bed in
one corner.

will came in and said, "honey, the doctor says you
have a bad infection and quite a lot of scar tissue on
the left side...."

"he did not say i could never have children, did
he?" my pale face begged for the right answer.

"no, but he said it might be difficult."

i drifted into sleep with will promising to come get
me first thing in the morning, and take me home.
it was one of the saddest nights of my life. shadows
moving across the walls. old paint. ugly linoleum
floors. my bed standing alone in all that gloomy
space, because the hospital was so crowded they
had no place else to put me.

it had all happened so fast. no time to pack a little
bag, put some makeup in. the next morning,
though i felt miserable, i stumbled to the bathroom
and splashed water on my eyes, taking the brush
out of my purse. i looked so colorless and bland
and empty-eyed in the mirror. because i always felt
my rejection in hawaii was a result of my
appearance, i was afraid dr. dyer would not accept
me when he saw how i looked the morning after.
even at that moment, i was fearful of rejection,
already so negative about myself for not coming
out with a better report.

dr. dyer could not have been kinder. he gave will a
prescription for a strong dose of antibiotics, told me
not to run for at least twelve days, and let me leave
for home.

no running for twelve days

not run for twelve days? IMPOSSIBLE. no way. i
would not be faithful if i did that. what did this
doctor know? in no uncertain terms, i informed
will i was going to do otherwise.

"ann, you are going to do what the doctor told
you!"

"no, i am NOT!" tears coming.

"i am your husband. i love you. you will give up
running for AT LEAST twelve days."

never, since i was a child, had i been back under
such authority. believing deeply in submission, i
could not totally ignore him and disobey, but
neither could i reconcile my not being faithful to
this discipline.

two mornings later, will stood by our bed before heading for the office.

"ann, remember, no running."

his face was sober. he meant it. he was a person most people wouldn't battle with. no one but me. i would not be afraid of him or overpowered by him.

it was the first time since we had married that will had said an unequivocal "no" to me. he gave me a lot of space. he had confidence in almost all my decisions. he was so secure in himself that he never seemed to need the reassurance of being in control of me.

he left for work, and the rage i felt inside was immense. no one was going to tell me what i could or could not do, especially with my running. yet i knew the quiet, deep conviction of my heart around the biblical admonition to "women, submit to your husbands." i had even put it into my marriage vows..."i submit to you as unto God...."

it was a major battle. finally, a great victory. i laid down this fierce, ugly fear of what might happen if i did not run...if i was not faithful to the regimen...to say "yes" to the call in my heart. once i resolved it, after several hours, i began to feel better. will was not an ogre. peace settled over me. for twelve days i rested and lay around, basically feeling too awful to do otherwise. it was only the start of a heartbreaking ordeal that would make where i was then look like elementary lessons further down the road.

months later, i learned that, had i run, my body probably never would have healed properly, creating much more scar tissue. surrendering had definitely been in my best interest. it had paid. what i didn't understand at this time was the relationship between my running achievements and my feelings of self-worth. to stop running was to cut away some of my own well-being.

infertility, a real problem

every month was a defeat.

in our little community in idaho falls, almost every
woman is a mother. our church has only seventy
members, but almost every other week it seems
another woman announces she is pregnant. babies
and toddlers and young children abound. being a
professional...coming from an east-coast
culture...was like moving a surfer to the antarctic.
i so wanted to be one with the women around me.
to identify. to share. but i felt odd and out of place
and lost amid the diapers and bottles and baby
cries. it was not their fault. it was my struggle.

many women have shared with me how they
almost hated those around them who were
pregnant or had babies. that it was a slap across
the face to what they were: infertile. not through
any of this can i remember that emotion surfacing.

i always felt excited about someone else's gift-on-the-way. sometimes, i wished it could have been me, but that did not affect my excitement for them. one of my favorite things was going to the maternity wards and seeing the new arrivals in the windows. buying and taking little baby gifts.

one day, i had been visiting, and happened to notice an exceptionally beautiful baby. it was not one i knew, but she was, in my mind, the loveliest baby in the entire nursery. i scrunched down, trying to read what room the mother was in, and went bounding in to this young woman, exclaiming my wonder over her baby. she seemed so pleased.

it was quite amazing. a few days later ryan div̶ a fabulous young potato farmer in our church, with three small children of his own, said, "ann, you met my sister, i hear."

"really? where?"

"at the hospital. she told my mom this lady came in and bragged on her baby, and we all knew it had to be you."

each month i counted the days. i took my basal temperature. dr. dyer had me on clomid, a fertility drug, to get me to ovulate. it took the strongest dosage before my body would respond. often because of the hormonal changes that come with clomid, it accelerated my emotions. when i knew my temperature went up, i would call will at the office: "honey, come home, i am OVULATING."

the pressure sometimes became almost destructive. one month, in particular, i had taken all my clomid. i had the two strong shots at mid-cycle to force the body to drop the eggs. i had done everything right. however, the intensity on my part to make this happen triggered something in will, and we had an all-out trauma. i was seething and sobbing. he became cold and distant. it remained that way for several days. by the time we came together, it was too late to try for a baby that month.

disappointment again

it was june, '82. i had just run my eighth marathon in duluth, minnesota. the doctor had increased my clomid to compensate for the added stress on my body. i wanted a baby desperately, but i could not relinquish the security that running brought me. they had done a simple but very painful procedure on me in the doctor's office. they had cut a tiny piece of my uterine lining, sent it to the lab, and in a few days would be able to tell whether i had actually ovulated. i was two weeks past my period, and my hopes were soaring.

until chicago. the airport. enroute from an appearance shortly after the marathon. i called the doctor long distance and his nurse, barbara, said, "ann, you cannot be pregnant. your test showed you did not ovulate." hopes dashed. tears stinging in my eyes. for years, lonely and struggling as i traveled the world trying to share God's and my

dreams, i had done major crying in airport phone
booths. it was the only place one could halfway
hide. be alone and private in such a rushing,
impersonal, almost intrusive place. all the tears of
the past, however, did not equal the pain of that
tremendous letdown, after trying for a full year
since i married. boarding the plane for idaho, my
heart was lead. my makeup smeared. the sky was
dark and waves of despair washed over me. i
would have to go home and tell will it had not
worked again.

will had waited thirty-eight years to marry. he
comes from a family with great pride built around
their strong heritage. he had often talked of "when
we have a child." i wanted desperately to bring the
firstborn grandchild into his family. somehow, in
my own way, to find a special place among them. i
desired to make will a father.

> "i will not doubt though all my ships at sea
> come drifting home with broken masts and
> sails;
> i will believe that hand which never fails,
> from seeming evil worketh good for me.
> and though i weep because those sails are
> tattered, still will i cry, while my best hopes
> lie shattered:
> i trust in Thee."

month after month, day after day, will would come
flying through the door. always so much energy
emanating from him. his face sort of flushed. his
dark eyes always flashing. life was terrific. we

were definitely on the edge of something great. every day was such an adventure.

"honey, it did not work again this month," i would choke out, my eyes searching his face.

"great, honey! thank the Lord. remember, He knows just what He is doing. in the right time, i know God is going to give us children. honey, i am the happiest man in the world. if you have five babies, i will be the happiest man anywhere. if you never have any, i still will be. i have YOU, and i am so blessed."

generally each month, no matter HOW hard i prepared myself for the worst, my hopes would rise. my heart quivering. waiting. grabbing on the thread of faith deep inside. over and over and over, the blows would come. the period would arrive. a feeling of defectiveness began to take over my thinking. for years, subconsciously, i knew it was there. now it was surfacing in a way i could not control. could not push back down inside. often, i felt shy and insecure about going anywhere in idaho falls. i was crippled. i was a failure in this area of marriage. who would want to spend time with me? still there were other spheres of life that brought joy. in boston. children from the little gym God had helped me build in the north end.

pablo...growing tall. still with the large, liquid brown eyes. the broken english. the heart that carried more dreams than most of the others.

little, fragile anna...now growing into adolescence. painting her fingernails and toenails. worrying about her hair. wearing shoes with little heels. still carrying the gentle smile. the searching eyes. her head tipped to one side with expression.

joseph...the charmer. black, flashing eyes. handsome face. lean, solid body. not very tall. exceptionally bright, but struggling in school. his mom, one of the MOST amazing women i know, has come to Christ in a deep, vital way. is trying to lead her family down the narrow but joyous way, with louis, her husband.

steve and debbie, gym directors, are now "four," having had another son last year. joshua, their eldest, seven years old, gets beat up daily by neighborhood bullies. they still live in a building infested with all kinds of creatures, but are continually trying to add little touches here and there. to make it more secure...more like "home."

every year, i still spend my speaking money to support the program. a few fellow dreamers, from all over the united states, are faithful contributors, and it makes the difference between ice cream this week or not. always, in each report from steve, there is growth on each level...primary, juniors, jr. high, high school, disciples' group, and parents' Bible studies.

the narrow dark street
with the bright, red door...

and the garbage down the sides, and clothes
draped across to
the next building. but the message is alive...
HE LIVES. Jesus really does...and love takes the
drab
and hollow and dirty and crowded...and makes it
beautiful.

outsiders, from all over the united states, have
come in to assist. ben zickefoose, from texas, comes
each year to do a stunt show. rhonda, from
indiana, and her teenagers, raised several thousand
dollars, and came to do a vacation Bible school for
two weeks, at their own expense. bob skaggs, an
expert craftsman, has driven across the country
from santa barbara, to do repairs. twylla, attending
a local college, comes weekly.

rainbows crawl through the alleys
and across the old bricks...and into big playrooms
and hearts with no songs...
and there is music.
God's own chorus of joy.

the last two summers, will and i brought the
children to idaho for at least a week. george loved
driving will's pickup in and out of the drive. we let
the children sleep in the backyard (they had never
seen a backyard, coming from the inner city of
boston). the first night, will, big and tough as he is,
instructed them NOT to get out of their sleeping
bags for ANYTHING. the next morning, they
walked in, drenched. they had obeyed, though our

underground sprinkler system came on at 4:00 a.m. and doused them thoroughly. will had forgotten about it. smile.

joseph spent awhile at chuck and karen wilson's, close to the ranch. they have a mine, and large, heavy equipment. rattlesnakes run wild there. one day, he rode his bike right into a rushing creek. memories forever.

we took the children down the snake river in rafts, and our friends had a cookout with chili and little cupcakes fixed right over the open fire. horseback riding and mountain climbing and fishing and camping out and finding a mcdonald's here and there. going down summer ski slopes in little

toboggans. guitars and ice cream and being invited
to people's homes for meals. swimming and a huge
water slide, and almost NEVER a worry about their
behavior. steve is terrific with them.

will and i held them on our laps. i fed them hot
cookies out of my oven. tucked them into bed. we
shared our struggles, our dreams. the children had
helped raise the money by hard work and
memorizing twenty-five Scripture verses. people
here contributed sack lunches and vans.

we sang. and laughed hard.
and cried.
and told deep secrets that needed to be shared
with someone who REALLY loves. i shared my
longing for a baby.
my tears of frustration. i kissed them. and
massaged their shoulders and watched will with
one boy on his lap and about six others listening to
each word, sitting around him.

it was hard to say good-bye again, to send them
back to their world...their mission...in boston; for
me to stay here in mine. to again see the pools of
tears in dark eyes. to wave until all the black heads
and strong, sturdy bodies were out of sight. to
come home to that separated place where i MUST
be. for them to remain in boston, in struggling
situations, is to make them strong. soldiers of the
Cross. it is to teach me that to really love is to give
away. to relinquish. to let God find a new mission
for me.

44

it is to wait until another summer when, Lord willing, they will come again. stronger. braver. with new comrades of the glorious faith beside them. running with us.

a round-the-world trip

we were leaving for a trip around the world. i had
twenty-five appearances to make in new zealand.
then we could visit various countries and have fun.
will was taking me to many places he had been
before, wanting to share them with me. we were
ecstatic when dear friends of ours, paul and
margaret pauley, accepted our invitation to join us.
with four grown daughters, they had many
grandchildren. they understood so much about life
and relationships and God's love. will and i loved
being around them. they were comfortable and
easy.

maybe i could conceive on this trip, in some exotic
part of the world. i had heard lots of stories about
women who took a trip and got pregnant after
many months of trying. something about the
altitude and the time change and shift in elements
outside the body.

it was my last weekend in new zealand. it had
been one of the most significant, unforgettable
experiences of our lives. being with bev holt, who
had put the whole package in new zealand
together. thousands of youth came to the rallies.
warm, vibrant people. we would drive or fly to
the next day's appearance, and sometimes i would
have speeches in two different cities in one day.
wonderful, but exhausting.

on that friday evening, i still had six presentations
to go, and i was on the edge. it seemed
overwhelming to me. paul and margaret and i had
gotten into the next town, and been taken by bev
and her secretary, margaret, to our motel. will was
doing business with shippers and growers in new
zealand where he had once done graduate studies.
he was to meet us at the motel in time to go with
us to the banquet of over a thousand where i was
keynoting that night.

first, i was worn out. though bev had worked out
an almost flawless schedule with rest and privacy
and good food each place, i had already spoken
nineteen times and did not think i could stand to
hear myself six more. saying nothing of the pity i
felt for all those forced to listen to me...especially
my husband and the pauleys and bev...like an old
record, stuck, playing over and over and over.

i would beg them to stay in their rooms and send
me out to the audience alone. it seemed such
punishment for them to come along. but they

stayed with me. will says it is like a good symphony. he can hear me over and over, and not get tired. smile.

second, the motel room was small and dark. will was nowhere to be found. i was a little frightened.

third, my secretary in idaho had just sent me, fresh off the press, a copy of my eighth book, I GAVE GOD TIME. though i knew what the manuscript was (i had WRITTEN it), i had not seen any of the pictures or the cover. as i flipped through the book, i saw my face flashed across different pages. i looked defective, it seemed. awful. stringy hair and too-sweet smiles. sort of tragic. and they had forgotten to put in a picture of me running! how could the editors have missed that? they took away my opportunity to remind the world that i was still physically strong, faithful to a dream. brave.

at this point, i began to cry uncontrollably. the whole world was dark, and i would never make it. all who read my latest book would feel sorry for how dowdy i had become since marriage. sorry for my lack of glamour. it so mattered to me that the book come across well because it was about will, and what if the world rejected him or my marriage? that was the most difficult part of the decision to marry will anderson. would the world accept him and love us?

finally, it was the end of the july cycle, and i failed again to make pregnancy happen.

when will walked into the room, typically alive and full of the wonder of life, he found me sitting in bed. paul and margaret on either side. i was in tears. with wrenching sobs. he had a dozen yellow roses in his hand and a questioning look on his face. whatever could be SO wrong? paul and margaret were saying, "oh, ann, please do not cry. we have never seen you cry like this. we cannot bear it. it will all be ok." it seemed too dumb to tell them the source of all my tears.

the pauleys slipped out, saying, "oh, will, we're so glad you're here." will crawled across the bed and wrapped me in his arms.

"honey, what could be so terrible?"

"i cannot speak six more times. i cannot stand my voice, and my period has come. and look at this book. oh, honey, i wanted it to be romantic and beautiful, and now the world will never think i am special again. they left out a running picture. all my life i was an athletic misfit, and now i cannot even remind anyone that i am not."

it was almost time to leave for the banquet hall. washing my face, i pulled on the same taffeta plaid suit i had already worn too many times, brushed my hair, and will quietly slipped me through the crowds to the head table. my eyes were swollen and somber. my heart twisted in pain, but believing as a child in God's love and plan.

I will not doubt though sorrows fall like rain,
and troubles swarm like bees about a hive.
i will believe the heights for which i strive
are only reached by anguish and by pain;
and though i groan and writhe beneath my
    crosses,
i yet shall see through my severest losses,
the greater gain.

there was still one more month for me to get
pregnant overseas. always, after so many days, my
faith would bounce back. a new month. another
chance. that dream would carry me until the next
defeat.

my exciting husband

will is the most exciting person to travel with i
have ever known. he does not believe in "tours,"
but rather hires cabdrivers and little old ladies on
junks in hong kong and gets people he would just
happen to meet along the way to take us places
tourists never go. money was not the issue. having
fun and experiencing life was. one cabdriver in east
germany even took us up to his tiny apartment
where he and his wife and eight–year–old
daughter all slept in one room. in india, a cabdriver
took us to a hindu burial site, where one body was
on the fire, and others were lying around, ready to
be next.

we were able to visit one of mother teresa's
orphanages for babies, through an indian
doctor…will nearly had to carry me away. i
became engrossed with these babies, carrying them

and cuddling them. in a moment, if he had approved, i would have taken an indian baby home with us. will had always wanted to go to red china, which we did, but our two favorite places were hong kong and istanbul. years before, will had visited istanbul and bought an exquisite, lacy negligee for the woman he would someday marry. he had kept it tucked away on a shelf for years, not telling anyone. on our wedding night, in boston, he had pulled it out. now we were visiting, husband and wife. it was romantic.

campus crusade people had been notified through our friend dr. bill bright. so had some nazarene missionaries, and that added a dimension nothing else could have. although we stayed in hotels downtown, often we were invited into their homes for a meal. they were terrific interpreters for us, also, and we took them along with us during the day.

in japan, one evening rather late, a young man, peter turner, had come to see will, basically on business. being a runner, he talked will and me into running five or six miles around the prince's palace, not too far from our hotel. the air was still and warm, and we began to fall into a comfortable pace, feeling the excitement of the city all around us. will suddenly said, "let's see if we can catch up to those people just ahead...." he had not been doing much running, and this "little" run was really beginning to wear him out. he wanted to get it over with as soon possible, and this seemed like a

good idea. i am always ready for a challenge, so i
darted out ahead of him and peter, running maybe
a six-minute pace, when my toe caught a rough
place in the pavement and i went flying, arms out,
face first, toward the asphalt. will was horrified.
he thought i probably had knocked out my front
teeth caps, which i had received after my bike
accident the summer before, and would have to go
toothless the rest of the way around the world.

sort of crying and whimpering, i had blood
running down my legs, my stomach, my elbows,
(fortunately, my face did not hit). will picked me
up, but i was determined to finish the run. our
pace considerably slower, we headed for the hotel
where will bought some terrible disinfectant and
INSISTED on pouring it into all my wounds. he
wanted NO infections. i cried harder then, and was
miserable for a week. we stayed in an exotic,
japanese inn in kyoto, where each room had a
private hot tub. getting into that water was
excruciating. every time will would touch my arm
or reach out for my hand or put his arm around
my waist, i would say "oh, honey, not there. that
hurts."

once in a while, reservations would get mixed up,
and in order to stay in the hotel, all four of us
would have to share a room. one night, our four
beds squeezed into a relatively small space, we
collapsed into sleep from sight–seeing and jet lag.
sometime much later, in the dark, i began to
awaken to paul's snoring. but there was a clicking

sound, also. i could not figure out what it was. finally, i rolled over and tried to focus my eyes in the dark room. there was will, his long arm straight up in the air, snapping his fingers, presumably trying to get paul to roll over. margaret, at that point, awakened, flew out of bed, and crawled into paul's single bed, rubbing his back and telling him not to snore. suddenly it was so hilarious, we started laughing uncontrollably.

we had arrived in germany, our last stop. the pauleys had left for home, and we were visiting our dear friends clark and anne, who were overseeing campus crusade for Christ in that country. they had been married fifteen years, and anne was forty. but the strong desire for children had never come before. earlier will and i had shared with them our feelings that faithful Christians should be raising tomorrow's leaders. they waited until we arrived to break the wonderful news that anne was three months pregnant. i WAS excited for them, but inside i felt sick and defeated. they had not even begun to try for a child when anne conceived. i was feeling more defective than ever.

for weeks, i had anticipated seeing clark and anne. they were the ones who had come to the united states and gone skiing with will and me. before we were married, it was clark who said, "i think i know men...and if there was ever a man in the world right for you, ann, it is will."

since our wedding fourteen months before,
however, all the change and transition had been so
difficult for me. i longed for their affirmation and
love and approval. now it seemed they were so
caught up with anne's pregnancy. the unborn baby
was all important. anne was where i longed to be:
bulging at the waistline with life inside. she had
really done it. she had conceived. she must be so
whole and special. my sense of self-worth
deteriorated even more.

we were visiting one of the quaint german towns,
and decided to stop for pizza at a small, round
table under the sky. suddenly, i felt the necessity to
run inside and ask for the ladies' room. oh, it could
not be my period! i was overdue, and if i could be
pregnant, then i would be where anne was. an
equal. not inferior. and i would be giving will a gift
beyond anything else i wanted to offer him.

a few minutes later, i walked out to our table and
smiled, looking as serene and happy as i possibly
could. inside, i was thousands of cracked little
strips of pain. the kind of pain that comes from
knowing you are hopeless, useless, no good. you
are nothing.

it was not until that night, checked into our hotel
room, that i threw myself across the bed, dug my
teeth into a pillow so no one could hear me, and
cried out, again, all the deep, paralyzing
disappointment. finally, under cool sheets, wrapped
in will's arms…my hair wet and sort of matted

around my tear-smeared face...i fell asleep and had
a few hours of relief. the next morning, sun
shining across our drowsy faces, i remembered my
dream. i knew it was not going to come to life in
some romantic setting overseas.

and i had so wanted it to!
to go home with the worthy feeling of having been
capable enough to make conception happen.

> "no chance hath brought this ill to me;
> tis God's own hand, so let it be.
> He seeth what i cannot see...
> there is a need-be for each pain.
> thou art the Workman, i the frame,
> Lord, for the glory of Thy Name,
> perfect Thine image in the same."
> (paul e. billheimer's book DON'T WASTE
>   YOUR SORROWS)

while we were in india, we stayed at the taj mahal.
marble and velvet and rich colors everywhere.
there were many fine places to eat right in the
hotel. hard to believe, when millions were living
down the streets around us, on the sidewalks,
literally, in abject poverty.

an exquisite outfit

walking through the lobby one evening, i saw in a
window a stunning, pure silk outfit of royal blue
with sequins and chinese collar.

"honey, you know how inexpensive things are
here. isn't that lovely! do you think i could just
inquire? i have really bought nothing on the whole
trip."

"sure...whatever."

it was a small shop. the narrow, silk pants and
sleek, smart, almost–dress–length top were a little
large. but they promised me they could alter it to
fit perfectly and have it ready before we were to
check out the next day. the price was so
conservative compared to what it would have been
in america, i was elated. my color. my style. from
india. but we told them we would let them know

the next day whether to alter it.

india was the only place in the whole world i had
ever desired to go. as a child, i read a book, "LET
YOUR HEART BE BROKEN BY THE THINGS THAT
BREAK THE HEART OF GOD." it gave me a
burning love for this country.

the next day, we went sight-seeing. by the time we
arrived back at the hotel, the little shop was closed.
i had hoped they might still be able to fix the
outfit the next morning, quickly, before we left.

it ended up being a rush checking out. horrible
flight departure time. pouring rain. trying to get a
cab for the four of us. (they were the smallest cabs
ANYWHERE. will was always the lucky one. being
the biggest, he got the front seat, while paul and
margaret and i were poured into the backseat,
bodies melting into one another, nearly suffocating
before we reached our destination.) will said it was
too confusing and crazy to try to get the dress
done. that i would have to forget about the outfit
now. we would find something nice later, along the
way.

i was DEVASTATED. somehow, it was in my heart.
something i just loved. after all, he dragged me
through every dark, dirty alley, up five flights of
steps often to a building jammed with shops.
always, he was looking for a better computer. finer

binoculars. the right wristwatch. japan. hong kong. bangkok. and i could not have my one lovely outfit?

i started whispering mean little words to him. over and over. about how thoughtless and inconsiderate he was. trying to make him feel as awful as i did.

it was late. steamy. i was weary. another long flight. seeing india had wrenched my most secure, quiet inner places. my heart, too, was broken by all we saw. i cried as we boarded our plane. it all seemed too much.

we arrived in dubai, next to saudi arabia. the wealthiest, most extravagant, high-priced spot on our entire trip. after checking into our beautiful hotel, i wanted to go soak in a hot tub of water. i had a hard time trying to feel clean after india. the memories of all the poverty kept plaguing me. all the sadness. the despair for millions. we were all going to a beautiful buffet downstairs for dinner in an hour or so. i was still sulking over the exciting, royal blue silk left in the little shop in india, never to be seen again. the people were probably furious with that american woman who promised to come back, and never did.

wrapping a towel around me, drying off, i walked out of the bathroom to say something to will.

"will…what do you think…?"
i stopped.

hanging there, on the closet door, was my outfit.
oh, it was dazzling. it was elegant. i was
STUNNED.

will smiled.
"you like it, honey? i went in and told them to
alter it, but that if you came back, to tell you it was
already sold. that i would pick it up. it was to be a
surprise."

all i could do was cry.
i was so happy.
so ashamed.
all those mean digs.
bearing down on him with my hurt.

i wore it to dinner that night. now, i pull it out of
my closet to wear for special occasions. it is so
much more valuable because of will's heart of love.
the boyish glee of surprise. the planned,
put-together gesture. i will never forget. i learned
something. not to take everything so seriously. to
let God be in complete control and not try to force
an issue either way.

on a roller coaster

month after month, will and i experienced the
roller-coaster emotions which are familiar to
couples trying to conceive a child. will experienced
them because i did. but he always seemed happy,
regardless. often he would come in. i would be in
the kitchen, preparing dinner, tears covering my
face. he would pick me up, carry me to the
bedroom, and hold me.

"oh, honey, it is never going to happen! are you not
sad? are you still happy you married me?"

always, he would laugh, and reassure me. he
helped me, over and over, to recover. he never did
or said anything to make me feel i was less than
what he had ever wanted.

one day, while visiting our close friends paul and

marie miller in washington, d.c., i had lunch with my friend patty. she was expecting her fourth child, and was around my age. naturally babies came up. what i had been through. infertility. she said something like this:

"ann, our family knows a world-renowned fertility specialist. he does intricate, extensive surgery so women can conceive. you must see him. well, that is, if i can get you in. he is very busy."

my face flushed and expressive, i ran into the millers' house to tell will. maybe this was the answer. what a miracle! now, if only patty could arrange it. a short time later, she called.

"ann, i reached dr. john marlow. he said he would be happy to see you, but was on his way out the door when i called, to catch a flight to boston. he has to lecture there tomorrow. when are you and will going to boston?"

"tomorrow...."

"well, here is his hotel phone number. he said to call him, and he would arrange a way to meet you there."

what an amazing, new friendship we found in dr. marlow. very warm. congenial. i immediately felt relaxed and valuable. he collected data. we visited. he had lectured the world over, on his specialty in

fertility–related surgeries. he grew up in IDAHO.
he had graduated from the same high school as
will, in blackfoot. they had several mutual friends.
had some of the same teachers.

"do you fly-fish?" john asked will.

will is a fly-fisherman from years back when he
and his dad would crawl through thick, wet
underbrush along the snake river…to spots no one
else knew existed…and eventually wade into the
stream, captivated and lost in some terrestrial
place, by the grandeur of it.

"well, i will come to idaho and let you take me
fishing," john smiled. we felt an immediate affinity
with this man. he said he was booked very heavily,
but would see what he could put together.

he had an opening february 4, and we took it. after
preliminary tests and minor surgery, he would
perform a five-hour surgery, cautiously and
intricately removing all scar tissue from around my
ovaries and tubes. he was exceptionally deft at
what he did, and he felt optimistic.

will and i flew to washington, d.c., and checked
me into columbia hospital for women, which was
his headquarters. what wonderful nurses he had: it
was an efficient, professional office. i felt relaxed,
but terribly frightened by surgery. would i have
the nightmarish reaction to the anesthesia again?

would i be very sick afterward? would i even make it through? i had heard horror stories of people wheeled into surgery with minor problems, expiring on the operating table. many women might not be afraid, but i was. all my childhood, we children were so healthy my mother never even had a thermometer around the house. hospitals were NOT my thing. but my desire for a baby overruled the fear and dread.

my private room was around a corner on the second floor, very small and plain. it was the night before surgery, and they were doing all the awful, undignified, embarrassing things to prep me. often a nurse would come in and ask will, "mr. anderson, would you feel more comfortable somewhere else? there is a waiting room around the corner."

absolutely not! he was not going to miss being with me. he stayed at my side with a stack of books, often with the telephone cradled to his ear, doing business, long distance. suddenly, a quiet knock, and who should walk in but dr. kenneth taylor, translator of *The Living Bible*, and his wife, margaret. our dear friends. they were attending a broadcasters' convention, heard i was in washington, d.c., and came by to have prayer with us. holding hands around my bed, dr. taylor prayed. God came and touched me with quiet peace and calm. will and i will never forget that beautiful gesture.

65

surgery was successful. an attending physician during the operation came in later to my room.

"mr. and mrs. anderson, i wish you could have watched dr. marlow. what a genius. i have never seen a doctor do so magnificently what he did. you are like new!"

i never felt nauseated. i do not remember recovery or even asking for pain medication, though they must have given me some. the nurses were wonderful.

at that time, however, i remember that two national christian magazines came out with will's and my pictures on the covers. my secretary had mailed them to me in the hospital for fun. will looked tough, somber, and overweight. i looked pale and pathetic in both. though i was quite heavily sedated, i sobbed. again, it hit some deep, overriding fear that my entire sense of value was wrapped up in how i looked, and now in what the world thought of will.

a nurse came rushing in with two percodan, strong pain medication, and said, "oh, ann, take these, you will feel so much better." her face was covered with worry.

no, i did not want pain medication. i cried all the harder. my pain was buried deep in my soul where only God and i could find it. finally, another nurse rushed in. "ann, we have dr. marlow on the phone. let's talk to him."

they led me down to the nurse's desk, and i proceeded to weep into the receiver.

"oh, john, i am so sad. the whole world is so dark...." he lovingly reassured me, and told will and me later that sometimes one can experience terrible postoperative blues. i still think it was those awful pictures on the magazines (it was not the magazines' fault! WE had sent the pictures). my reaction to them was the problem, however. it showed me how much self-doubt was buried in my psyche.

will had to return to idaho after the first week, but it was necessary for me to have complete rest and no travel for two more weeks. staying with paul and marie is always great fun. she is one of the best cooks in the whole world, besides. after will left, an incredible snowstorm hit the east coast, and for seven days we could not get out of the house. even paul, chief of ceremonies for the white house, stayed home. marie and i lay in their bed and listened to tapes. there were moments when i had this ever-so-subtle nagging pain in the lower left side of my back. but i thought nothing of it. other moments i did not feel quite right, but after all, i was recovering!

new hope

it was difficult to be apart from will, so when i
flew home it was with tremendous anticipation.
the future looked so promising. surely a baby
would soon be on the way. i was going to be back
in my little home with my fine husband.

three days after my return, i became violently ill.
will rushed me to pocatello and dr. dyer. through
blood tests, he discovered i had a serious,
high-grade infection and said, "ann, we MUST
hospitalize you. feed you strong doses of antibiotics
intravenously. otherwise, you will undo the
surgery."

the doctor knew dr. marlow. had also read some
articles in medical journals by him. had great
respect for him, and delight that i should be able to
have him care for me.

to be admitted to the hospital! that was overwhelming to me. i refused. i had had a month off from speaking, but friday night (and this was already thursday) i was to speak in tampa, florida. there was no way i could cancel. i was not dying. with earnest begging, i asked dr. dyer to give me whatever medicine i could take by mouth and release me.

a quiet thought suddenly came to me. maybe will could go to florida in my place. he was articulate, far more brilliant, relaxed. i carefully presented the idea to will, and he, wanting so much for me to remain in the hospital, said, "ok...if the sponsor wants me. but, ann, i am a businessman and a potato farmer and i am ONLY doing this for you."

it was march 14, 1983, an EXACT year later since i had been admitted to the same hospital for that emergency surgery.

will, in the course of several months, addressed five different audiences for me so that i would stay in bed, and every sponsor would not be left in a terrible predicament. the crowds, from tampa to dallas and minneapolis and portland, loved him. we began receiving fan mail at my office for HIM.

he would fly home, and i would say,
"honey, how did you do?"
"ok. just did my best." that was all. but the enthusiastic reports poured in.

while home, recovering from losing eighteen pounds and trying to regain my strength, i conceived. during this period of convalescence, it never occurred to me even to try, i was so focused into getting well. there were several days when i became very nauseated and predicted i had caught a flu bug from my weakened state. dr. julian debruynkops, our dearly loved internist, and don dyer had decided to do some xrays of my kidneys because i felt so awful, but insisted on a pregnancy test first. xraying the abdominal cavity, when i had not yet had a period, concerned them. the night before, my stomach churning in that familiar way with expectation, i began to spot. i KNEW this would happen. it always did. it was as if God stuck a carrot under my nose, over and over, and just as i would about grab it, He would snatch it away. will was out of town that night. i called jan, as i had for many months, completely broken.

then i crawled into bed and began singing all the old, faithful hymns i could remember learning as a child, crying out as i sang. and praising God because i knew that was what i was supposed to do, even though it took great determination. i felt i was beginning to embarrass even the doctors. failure covered the walls, and sadness.

however, the next morning my temperature was still up, and no period had come. i drove to pocatello for the blood test, not telling anyone. not even will. it was humiliating enough just to subject myself to this disappointing test.

conception

the suspense was almost more than i could handle.
i stumbled around the house praying for courage.
begging. when the phone rang, i froze. picking up
the receiver, i said "hello" with a flat voice.

"ann, this is barbara. how are you?"
"fine...." cautious. steeled. barbara was dr. dyer's
nurse.
"dr. dyer wants to speak to you."

my heart began screaming with an excitement i
could hardly contain. barbara always told me when
the report was negative, but now she was putting
the doctor on!

"ann...your test is positive."

tears streaming. sunshine across the floor. a song
somewhere in the distance. one broken, weak

heart made joyful. Jesus did pay. He did. He did.

it was wednesday. the night of our Bible study-growth group. dinner was ready when will walked in. we sat down and he looked at me with a strange questioning in his eyes.

"are you all right? everything ok?"

i smiled.

"would you like to hear something really beautiful?"

"sure...shoot!"

"i am pregnant." eyes shining. face pink from excitement.

will jumped up, grabbed me, and began to twirl me around and around. i had not been feeling too well anyway, and that made me feel worse.

but i was too HAPPY for anything to bother me.

we went to our little growth group. at the close, will said, "ann is going to have to be admitted to the hospital for a serious procedure...."

everyone became very grave. they knew i had been so ill. now what?

"you will have plenty of time to pray, however. it

will not be for eight months."

the realization crept over them. the shock and
surprise. astonished, happy faces. warm hugs. i
was not a freak. i was not defective. i had done it.
with God and will. alleluia. alleluia. amen.

emergency

we loved calling our families and closest friends
and sharing the news, but the joy was short-lived.
soon after, an ultrasound showed some kind of
abnormality. i was in my office, dressed to fly, my
bags with me. will was accompanying me to
minneapolis where i was to speak to a sellout
crowd, and visit our friends helmut and bev
wenshau. though i had a pain in my lower back, i
had assumed it was part of pregnancy, and felt i
must go on. suddenly, my phone rang. dr.
debruynkops was on the line. (we call him julian.)

"ann, i have conferred with john marlow and don
dyer and we all agree you must go immediately to
pocatello and let don run some tests. possible
surgery is involved. we are fearful of a tubal
pregnancy or some other complication. ann,
nothing is as important as this. your life is at stake.
you MUST DO IT."

it was 4:00 p.m. our flight left in forty minutes.
will was trying to finish up last-minute details. i
flew into his office and into his arms, a terrified
look on my face. pam, my secretary, was busy
calling my agent and the sponsor in minneapolis.

"will, something terrible has happened. julian says
i must go see don and probably be put into surgery
immediately," i wailed. no more shining eyes. tears
and a terrified expression spread across my face,
my body trembling.

wonderful, strong will. never flustered. never
unnerved. never out of control. in charge. no fear
apparent. so calming. "honey, you must do as julian
says...."

pam buzzed his line.
"will, minneapolis is begging for you to come on.
they are sold out and do
not know what they will do without you...."

so tough. i wanted him with me. yet i could not
bear to disappoint the crowd. we decided he must
go.

pam raced me an hour away to dr. dyer. will
caught his flight through salt lake city and on.
during his layover, he called my room at the
hospital. they had just brought me in. the
anesthesiologist was standing by my bed, ready to
inject something into my vein. "honey, i am in salt
lake. how are you?" that deep, steady voice. i was

hysterical under the surface. trying to be subdued on the level that showed.

"will, i am so scared. i need you. honey, please do not let them take me into surgery again. not another cold room and putting that frightening mask over my nose and the lights spinning. my trying to stay awake. do not let them do this to me."

"ann, let me speak to the anesthesiologist."

"dr. sullivan," said his little name plate. i handed the receiver to him. he was a striking man, but had been very matter-of-fact and aloof until that point.

"dr. sullivan, this is will anderson. some turkey gave ann the wrong anesthesia at your hospital about a year ago. i do not want it to happen again. will you be sure to research her records and make the appropriate change?"

as the doctor put the receiver down, there was a kindness and gentleness about him that seemed to reach out to me. as if suddenly he understood how afraid i was. how much i had already suffered. in that instant, he became my friend, and was there holding my hand when i awakened in recovery, instantly aware of how sick i was. how awful suffering could be.

"ann, this is dr. dyer. i am here with you, too. it

was not tubal. you have a normal pregnancy. there
was a cyst and a lot of infection. try to be brave,
and we will hope you can carry this pregnancy."

they brought pam right into the recovery room,
knowing how alone i felt. i was in so much pain i
hardly wanted to live.

he had said the baby was ok.
i would fight. be brave. overcome.

"ann, i was so scared when i saw you," pam told
me later. "your face was white as a sheet and your
lips all swollen."

it was hours before they found a medication that
finally relieved my pain. my body responds poorly
to many of them. pam slept on the linoleum floor,
on a blanket, right by my bed, all night. she never
left me. will stood before a filled auditorium and
shared his heart, not knowing what had happened
to me. he led them all in prayer for me.

for a week, i was ordered to stay in bed in my
private hospital room, allowed to get up only for
the bathroom. though they gave me some
medication, they had to be cautious with the
pregnancy factor. the fresh incision from one side
of my abdomen to the other had been opened only
six weeks before for the surgery in washington. it
was still tender when they had to open me this
second time. constant cramping. the doctor urging

me to EAT, but i was so miserable that food did not appeal to me. i did try.

so often that previous week, someone (usually pam) would wheel me, wearing a gown and robe, down to the nursery to watch the babies. people would ask, "which one is yours?"

"oh, not any of them. mine is in here," proudly pointing to my tummy.

pam and i would study all the tiny faces through the glass. watch as friends and family exclaimed. pick out the new ones each day. i loved babies. they were the most wonderful gifts that i knew in the world, and God was now going to let me have one, too.

in a couple of days, i was to speak to a thousand ladies in dallas at the anatole hotel, and to several hundred others in another location. tickets were already sold. everyone waiting. when my agent called to cancel, the sponsors panicked. could will come? again, a dilemma. he had several businesses to run. i was so ill. we again decided he should go.

"ann, i do not want to stay at the hotel. let them know. i will go to bruce and georgia's."

it was so hard to see will leave. everything was so tentative.

often, during the noon hour or some unexpected

moment, dr. sullivan would stop by and chat. he had done some running. he was fascinated by the story of will's and my meeting. i loved to have him visit.

one evening, several days before he flew to dallas, will was sitting by my bed when dr. sullivan peeked in. we coaxed him to come sit a minute.

"by the way, will, i went back through all the records to find out who that 'turkey' was who did ann's anesthesia a year ago. the turkey was i. i wanted you to know. i will see to it that it does not happen again by me or anyone else in charge."

we were amazed by his honesty. we loved him all the more. our confidence in him soared.

will flew to dallas on thursday, a windy, cloudy day in april. i was lying alone in my room, very afraid. there was some fever and spotting, and nothing looked very good. suddenly, in the door walked my mother and pam. will had decided i needed my mother. here she was. a great surprise. a comfort. my parents had prayed many hours for will and me, through all this, and it almost seemed harder on them than on us, to watch us suffer. my heart was still heavy. the misery in my body could not equal what was in my trembling spirit.

miscarriage

around 7:30 p.m. dr. dyer walked in. examined me.
gave a grave, sad look. "ann, you are miscarrying. i
am going to have you prepped for surgery."

he walked out. my mother entered, and i threw
my arms around her. "oh, mom, it is over. i am
losing the baby. all the pain and courage for
nothing."

we cried together as the nurses rushed in, put a
clean gown on me, got me in a wheelchair, and
headed me toward the elevator. the doomed place
called "surgery." one of the nurses at the front
station walked around the corner to me and
wrapped her arms around my neck. i buried my
face in her white, fresh uniform, and cried some
more. "honey, i am so sorry. you will be back to
deliver another one. you will see."

dr. dyer decided to use an emergency room for me
since all the delivery rooms were full. they
wheeled me past several doors where horrible,
guttural screams were pouring out. several people
with overdoses had come in that night, dr. dyer
explained, and they were being revived. i had
never heard any human sounds so awful, and
already the world was darker and more lonely
than anything i had ever imagined. my eyes kept
filling with tears. it was a nightmare. all of it. don,
and the attending nurse, cheryl, were kind, gentle,
subdued.

dr. dyer laughed later. "ann, you were great
entertainment, wandering in and out of sleep,
talking. you thought i was your agent. 'do not let
them book me one more date! i mean it. not one
more.' " he said he would reassure me, but a few
minutes later i was making him promise again.

there is nothing else i remember about that night
but awakening in my own room, crying out in
pain. the nurses brought me two percodan, but i
was frantic. "oh, please," i begged. "that will not
be enough. it will not work." could they not give
me a shot?

"ann, dr. dyer said you stopped breathing a couple
of times on the table and he wanted us to watch
you very carefully."

my mother held me in her arms, crying, while i
cried. she told me later it was almost more than

she could handle to see me suffering so. finally,
they did give me a shot. they led my mother to an
easy chair down the hall where she could sleep.
pam asked for another sheet and pillow and took
her customary place by my bed on the hard, cold,
linoleum floor. her depth of love for me through
all this was unmatched. there is nothing in the
world that i can think of i would not do for her the
rest of my life.

meanwhile, in dallas...

in dallas, several thousand miles away, will had to face these two large groups of women, knowing the story back home. our friend bruce told me will buried his head in his hands and wept....knowing will anderson NEVER cried, i realized the whole trauma was taking its toll on him, too.

next morning, pam and my mother headed for the coffee shop. the doctors were going to let me go home. i crawled out of bed, washed my hair, showered, and wandered into the hall as the nurses were bringing all the newborns, pink and blue bows glued on their heads, to their mothers. they looked too beautiful and sweet. so tiny. i felt so alone. black clouds and showers of sorrow washed over and through me.

there was a choice. to make sorrow my friend or my enemy. to walk with it and let it teach me, or scorn it and become bitter.

george watson says, "God uses for His glory those
people and things which are most perfectly
broken. those who are broken in wealth, broken in
self-will, broken in their ambitions, broken in their
beautiful ideals, broken in worldly reputation.
broken oft-times in health. these are the ones the
Holy Spirit is seizing upon and using."

i began to sing softly,
"i have had many joys and sorrows...questions
about tomorrow...sometimes i
feel so all alone...
but in every situation, He gives blessed consolation,
that the sorrows come to only make me strong...."
(andraè crouch).

i knew sorrow could unfold to me things nothing
else ever had. i decided to open my arms to it. to
let it be my teacher. sorrow took the fluff and
sham out of my life. smoothed many rough edges.
taught me better who God is and who i am not.
began to fill my life with new softness. with
compassion. i learned how to understand more
authentically the crying world around me. and
how to celebrate with the joy of realizing the value
of the gift.

for years i had said to audiences:
"Jesus is love and love is good, and love changes
even the most difficult into
something beautiful."

now was my opportunity to live it out. to prove
what i believed was true.

to love is to be vulnerable. to open one's life and let
God take out or put in anything He wants.

> "measure thy life by loss and not by gain
> not by the wine drunk, but by the wine
>   poured forth.
> for love's strength standeth in love's sacrifice,
> and he who suffers most has most to give"
>   (henry ward beecher).

God took my longed-for baby to fulfill His supreme
aim of building my character and making me
whole.

driving back to idaho falls that day was sad. no
more baby. the dream dead. the few little baby
gifts brought to the hospital in a sack in the trunk.
will was not home yet. my struggle to feel secure
in this new corner of the world became all the
more intense. why had we called so many, so soon,
about the pregnancy? now we would have to let
them all know it was over. i felt embarrassed. there
WAS something defective about me.

the hope chest

on a tuesday night. will's and my time to be
together. alone. i was leaving early the next
morning to address a convention in indiana. i
would be away for five days.

my secretary, pam, asked me to come to her house
that night. she said she had something to give me.

"oh, pam, i don't know. it's tuesday...i'll try."

will said we should go.

when we arrived, pam took me to her bedroom.
there stood an old battered antique chest of
drawers. she said, "ann, i've heard you tell the
story of how you filled a little chest when you
were a girl. and how you had so much faith then. i
thought maybe we should begin to fill this chest of

drawers...in faith...for your and will's babies. i
need you to help me."

pam had looked at all the garage sale ads in the
newspaper, hoping to find an inexpensive chest.
she had phoned friends to see if they might know
of something. someone overheard pam's
conversations and offered to give her an old chest
which was being stored in a basement...glad to get
rid of it. they loaded it in a pickup truck and,
drawer by drawer, pam hauled it off to her room.
she bought some diapers and washcloths and baby
powder and soap to put in the drawers.

pam had written all the stores where i shop in
boston and dallas and san francisco. she told them
the story of the chest. she asked if they would like
to help us fill the little chest with the finest, the
loveliest and most beautiful things.

will and pam and i stood in front of the old chest
of drawers. put our hands on it. and prayed, if God
so willed, that he would bless us with children.

(will said it would be our hope chest.)

several days later, chuck and karen stopped in with
a beautiful strawberry pie. they were the first
people i had met in idaho. their place was not far
from the ranch, and will had loved them for years.
now i did, too. the pie was to fatten ME, but will
cleaned up most of it. my body had been through
such an ordeal that my appetite was almost nil.

another evening, our neighbors chuck and carol came by. he is a deacon in their church, and carol and i used to run together. she had a new heating pad wrapped for me. we held hands and chuck prayed. i will never forget what i felt that night. love engulfing my shattered spirit, and keeping some tiny thread of hope alive.

glen, will's overseer at the ranch, would call and send flowers more than once. my mother-in-law kept the refrigerator stocked, and me in beautiful nightgowns. people in our church were so kind, often bringing dinner for will and me each evening. for weeks, i did not feel good, no matter how hard i tried. for the most part, i stayed in. took frequent naps. read book after book. pam would bring mail and business from the office. there were still a lot of antibiotics to take, and i was very anemic.

a deeper "yes" than ever before

one night, will and i were lying in bed, lights out,
when an overwhelming sense
of despair began to fill me. once i started crying, i
could not stop. will
would kind of rock me.
"honey, sing something," i would choke out.
what i had in mind was a beautiful hymn like
"trust and obey" or "through it
all." the only songs he could think of were his old
fraternity songs, hoping
they would make me laugh again.
"ho...ho...ho...hannah...my delta gamma...
i put my arms around as far as they will
go...go...go...."

i cried all the harder. in my mind i began to
ponder all the pain my body had been through. the
hundreds of needles. the cold, impersonal operating
rooms, the dreadful memories of awakening in

recovery rooms. listening to others all around me
screaming. shaking and hurting and no one
seeming to be nearby to care. the memories would
not leave me. my body curled into a little ball,
crying more violently. will rubbing my back.

"ann, honey...take a breath. it is all right."

i was crying so hard at moments i did not breathe.
it was not sorrow, really, over the baby's loss. that
took me a long time to work through. this was for
brokenness of my poor body. for me. for all we
had been through.

> "whole, unbruised, unbroken men are of little
> use to God...because they are deficient in
> agape love" (j.r. miller).

suddenly, will jumped up and headed for the
kitchen. i knew immediately what he was going to
do. get me vitamins! whenever i was not feeling
well, he would hand me a slug of big, awful pills,
and say, "honey, take these. you will feel much
better."

i went flying into the kitchen after him.

"no, will, i will not take vitamins," i wailed. "they
never help me and they certainly will not now."

standing under the kitchen light, i saw will. his
face covered with my mascara. smeared across his
white tee shirt, too. i began to laugh. he was so tall

and strong and in earnest...and had black smudges everywhere.

"will, call earl lee. i just want him to pray for me." former nazarene missionary to india, he and his wife, hazel, were two of my most respected Christian friends. next to my dad, i counted most on earl's prayers.

we headed for bed again, and i jumped in, exhausted. spent. will knelt by the bed. immediately, i rolled over and down next to him.

"Father God," he prayed, "it seems as if ann and i have had all we can handle. it has been tough. but we only go through life once. we want all you can have for us. do not ease up. do not quit if you see we need more...."

at first, i felt horror. "do not ease up...." how much more could i handle? with my pale, small hand clasped in will's big, strong one, i said "yes" to God, too. to a deeper "yes" than ever before.

in september, i flew to washington, d.c., to have dr. marlow laparoscope me (a tiny incision made in the navel where they put a camera through and can see the abdominal cavity). we wanted to know what all the infections had done to his long, intricate surgery. to know where to go from there. ron and nancy, two of our closest friends, looked after me. ron had a marvelous chauffeur, ed, take nancy and me to the hospital. i was to be released

late that evening, and ed would wait the six hours
or so, and bring us home. he was a radiant
Christian and assured me he would be praying.

another emergency

again, i had a strong reaction to the anesthesia. will had called ahead, trying to ensure the right anesthesiologist. but it is such a busy place, and someone i had never seen before administered it. i am allergic to only one thing i know of: composine. anything with even a derivative of it affects me. at midnight, i was absolutely begging john marlow to let ed and nancy take me home. it was to be a simple procedure, but typically, for me, it became a nightmare. i told will on the phone that i would NEVER let anyone take me to surgery again. i would choose death first. i meant it.

two days later, i was supposed to go home, but my abdomen began swelling to about a fifth-month pregnancy size. ron and nancy quickly took me, on a sunday afternoon, to john's office, where he was waiting.

"ann, i think you are hemorrhaging. we have got
to prep you for surgery. we cannot wait."

"no, john, no!" i sobbed. "please. i will die instead.
i do not mind."

throwing my arms around nancy in the hall, i
cried and cried. ron headed home to bring back
anything i needed. john called will, but it was
already late afternoon, and there was no way he
could fly across the country in time. john spoke
with him for thirty minutes or so, answering as
many questions as he could. we were SO thankful
we had john marlow. laurie, sixteen, hurriedly
baked chocolate chip cookies for ron to bring.
nancy sat on my bed and read me psalms as they
got me ready.

looking at the lovely nurses as they rolled me
down the hall, my eyes swimming with tears, i
began to sing:

> "oh, let the Son of God enfold you with His
> wonder and His love. let Him fill your life and
> satisfy your soul. oh let Him have the things
> that hold you, and His spirit like a dove, will
> descend upon your life and make you whole."

"honey, you do not have to be afraid," one nurse
with a strong accent assured me. "dr. marlow is
one of the best in the world."

God took care of everything. john marlow made

sure the right anesthesia was administered. it was discovered that i was not actually hemorrhaging, but had some very irritated places, and he did not have to make the incision as large as he had feared.

i flew home completely broken. there never seemed to be an end. how much could one person handle? ron and nancy had been so loving and good to me, and i was bonded to them in the most intimate sense. they had walked this painful road beside me.

more and more, i began to realize something our dear friend bob had told me. "ann, God is your Source. this thing is too hard for humans, no matter how skilled they are. trust and reaffirm your faith in your Source. and begin to thank God for what HE is getting ready to do."

trusting God is not always easy

how hard, sometimes, to trust God. to believe He really loved me so much He would not withhold good things from me. to give up control. to quit trying to do it myself. to be stripped, more and more, of all one's false securities and stand little and naked and scared before almighty God. to return to the only true Hope. to let the dream die. to…

> "give what he cannot keep to gain what he cannot lose" (jim elliot).

oswald chambers, in MY UTMOST FOR HIS HIGHEST, says:

> "as long as you have a personal interest in your own character, or any set ambition, you cannot get through into identification with God's interest. you can only get there by losing forever any idea of yourself and by

letting God take you right out into His
purpose for the world, and because your
goings are of the Lord, you can never
understand your ways.... i have to learn the
aim in life is God's, not mine. God is using me
from His greatest personal standpoint, and all
He asks of me is that i trust Him, and never
say, Lord this gives me such a heartache. to
talk in that way makes me a dog. when i stop
telling God what i want, He can catch me up
for what He wants without hindrance. He can
crumple me or exalt me, He can do anything
He chooses. He simply asks me to have
implicit faith in Himself and in His
goodness...."

after getting back into the routine of home life, i
began trying to grow stronger. spending good
times with God, early hours in His Word. one day
we invited a family over for dinner. they grow
potatoes on will's ranch. vernon and beulah martin,
and their married daughter and son. it so mattered
to me that it be a fun evening. i felt a little
uncertain because vernon is an authentic,
thoroughbred farmer. will wears white shirts and
ties and pinstripe suits to the office. vernon wears
overalls and suspenders. the real mccoy. i had had
the flu for a week before, so will had gone to
wendy's and bought hamburgers and baked
potatoes for everyone. i had heard these
magnificent stories about farm wives and their
steak and gravy and hot biscuits at 5:00 a.m., and i
felt very embarrassed and foolish, but i still so
wanted them to come. vernon had farmed on the
ranch since the beginning, and will loved him. i

wanted to get better acquainted.

putting my loveliest taffeta place mats on the table, i piled the potatoes on one silver tray, and the hamburgers on another large silver platter. cold drinks. hot, brewed coffee. i had made cheesecake (a recipe from jan boston, one of the FINEST cooks i know) for dessert. a roaring fire. burning candles. i got on my knees in our closet, apron tied around my waist.

"Jesus, i know it is just wendy's for dinner. something i have NEVER done before. but what really matters is Your presence.
Your love. visit with us and laugh with us."

we had such fun. vernon and will talked potatoes, and i hardly understood any of the statistics. my sister, jan, was visiting, and she sat next to beulah and chatted. their children, in their late twenties, had been married ten years, and had not been able to have children. we had so much in common. so many emotions to share. they were a lovely couple with so much to give a child. and vernon would have been a wonderful grandfather like you read about in old-fashioned stories: wonderful!

suddenly, this idea came to me. let's hold hands around the table and pray for a baby for this couple. i did not even know what or how they believed, but i knew all about impossibilities and dreams and miracles and a giant God. will and i were standing beside them. running the same race.

will had prayed for dinner. i prayed for the baby.

when i finished a simple prayer, a touch of magic seemed to flash across my mind. my eyes filled with tears, i told them about our little "hope" chest.

"i want you to have something from our chest…in faith for your baby."

i ran to the little room, opened the drawers, studied everything. pulling out my favorite little gown with its matching hat, i folded it and brought it out.

"oh, ann, i am going to put it under my pillow and believe, too."

hamburgers and cokes and potatoes and cheesecake. shop talk and small talk and wood crackling in the fireplace. shattered dreams and smashed hopes. tough potato seasons and no babies. but LOVE. and belonging. and hope reborn. and a baby's gown tucked under a pillow, by a mother's faith, in hope of a miracle.

would we want to adopt?

a call came to my office, completely unsolicited. it was a family service in idaho falls. a baby was to be born in a couple of weeks. would we be interested? there were other families ready to take the baby, but word had reached them that i miscarried and had had problems, and they felt we would make wonderful parents. the baby would be interracial, a mixture of black skin and hair, and blond, blue-eyed Norwegian. i had always wanted an interracial baby. if only i could talk will into this. (i had not learned total relinquishment.)

"honey, you know how deeply we feel against abortion. this is our chance to champion the cause. to stand against it. to be a healing force."

will tried to be open, but he was, nevertheless, hesitant.

"go ahead and tell them we will come to the initial meeting, then we'll decide there. remember, ann, you have been awfully sick."

we met kirk, the psychologist, in his office. about our age, he was warm, gregarious. frankly, i had hardly known the office was there, one floor below ours in the same building.

there did not seem to be any negative family history. no alcoholism or hereditary illnesses. the mother was young. the father out of high school, working. we signed the sheet, stating we had met, and agreed to proceed. though we had never discussed adoption (the doctors remained optimistic for me), i began to feel bonded to this unborn child. mixed blood. the child would probably be beautiful. after growing up in hawaii, hating my white skin next to everyone else's creamy tans, i was thrilled at the prospect of having a child like that.

a baby. a tiny newborn. we would go to the hospital ourselves and get the baby. i began to visualize it. to daydream about it. God had wiped His loving Hand across the dark sky and left a big, shining place. joy, when least expected, can come in the morning. i heard a song on the edge of my heart for the first time in over a year.

"ann, i think we should seek people's advice," will began. "this is a major issue. you have been so ill.

frankly, i think the timing's off."

"honey, i need a baby. 'joy doeth good like medicine.' if anything can help me, this could," i pleaded.

will approaches life so differently from me. things are academic and systemized and intellectually analyzed. basically, i operate not so much on the empirical level, but the intuitive. by my gut feelings. besides, it seemed that God had opened this door for us.

calls were made to relatives. to close friends. to doctors. we took our internist to lunch. my idea. he knew as well as anyone what i had been through. we wanted to see what he would say.

"ann and will, if the baby has been thoroughly tested out to be healthy, i think it is just what you need. ann will blossom and probably have five children of her own."

if will was talking to someone on the subject, he always emphasized the health issue. "i am really concerned about ann's health...."

reacting, rather than giving it to Jesus, i would become paralyzed with fear. what if others agreed with him? he already had a doctor's positive opinion. what more did he need to worry about?

when i called people (though initially this was will's idea), i would immediately bring up the health issue, but quote my doctor's words, and try to influence them to my persuasion.

somewhere, deep inside, i knew submission to will was going to be a major issue. we were on two tracks moving toward opposite points, and something cataclysmic was going to happen.

marital agreement is not always easy

one night, kirk came to our home to talk with us.
to help will make a decision. i had never known
will not to be decisive. though he could not seem to
articulate his doubts, he said there were some, and
he did not feel open to it. knowing how seriously i
was hoping for this baby...having a great deal of
faith in my own basic intuition...created a huge
precipice for him.

we soon forgot the baby, and kirk was working
with will and me. there was something at stake in
our marriage. something that was not right in the
way we were relating to each other. he helped us
understand that through all the transition and
change in my life, and my always wanting to
please and be the perfect wife, i had lost a sense of
myself. will is authoritative, commanding. a deep
place in me had gotten totally lost under that. a

little baby represented companionship to me, for the long hours will was away. a solution, not to our marriage, but to a dying part of me. if we took the baby, it was still important that we work on us. on my becoming more assertive, on will's backing off and letting go.

will finally said, "go ahead and fix the nursery. we will eventually use it one way or another. the light, for now, is green." i was exultant.

the nursery was readied. white crib. a bassinet for our room. the little chest with some exquisite things i had bought in exciting stores in faraway cities while on speaking trips. a rainbow on the wall and a little bear my mom had sent. a gorgeous, hand-knitted yellow blanket from my mother-in-law, jo. a fetching little doll made by gladys ream, jan's mother-in-law.

"ann, this is kirk"…his voice breathless. "the mother has gone into labor."

i squealed. it was almost as if it were i. today was the day a baby would be born. maybe for us.

"ann, how about a little girl? six pounds. the doctor says beautiful and healthy."

will arrived home that night and i threw my arms around his neck. "it is a girl, honey. a little girl."

he looked down into my blue eyes with sort of an "oh, God-what-am-i-going-to-do" look. "really, that is interesting."

from the beginning, we had different attitudes. i wanted this baby so badly. it would bring back some deep lacking in me. will did not feel ready, so quickly, for a baby. he liked the idea of nine months to prepare. throughout, we both tried very hard to hear the other out. to find mutuality. to be sensitive. it WAS a major decision. yet i saw all the "yeses." will felt the "nos." i wasn't that sure about submission. why would will make a better decision than i?

questioning will; questioning God

The day before we were to get the baby, will said, "ann, i just don't feel right about adopting this baby at this time."

"it is your decision," i coughed out. "you have to feel right about it. you had better call kirk so he can notify someone else." the crushing bomb had hit.

in my whole life, i had never felt that devastated. i closed the door to the nursery, and took my pillow and a blanket to the couch. i did not know what i felt for will anderson. there was no mutuality in that decision. but then, in submission, mutuality is not even an issue. will went to bed, and a couple of hours later when i went in and found him sleeping, i was enraged. how could he fall asleep so easily, when he had just left me with another funeral experience! i awakened him, screaming. finally, in the kitchen, he wrapped his arms around me tightly, and though i tried hard to free myself, he would not let me. he kept saying, "ann, i love you so much. do you know how hard it is to say 'no' to you?"

my body began to quiver and shake with sobs that were uncontrollable. pain poured out of me as water from a faucet. he picked me up and carried me back to bed, where i cried for hours. i could even feel the pain in my toes. the sorrow wracked my body. again, a carrot. again, God pulling it away from me. a mean trick. He could not love me. i had always thought He did, but now i knew how wrong i had been. i would not do to a worst enemy what He had allowed for me the last two years.

at one point, i felt will's body shaking. he was crying, too. it frightened me. he did not cry. not even at his father's funeral. men, he was told, do not do that. yet here he was. i did not want to make him feel as awful as i did. at least, not consciously. we finally fell asleep under a clouded sky, with a little room closed off at the end of the hall. i awakened over and over, crying myself back to a drowsy sleep. if i had carried that baby in my womb nine months, and lost her, i do not believe i could have felt any more grief.

friends came from salt lake, bill and penny. we all

went to sun valley for the weekend. will rented an
exotic, gorgeous condominium, and we played.
there was some peace in me. it had hurt more, i
decided, before i knew the outcome. fearing what
it would be. hoping against hope. now that was
over. no matter how devastating the answer might
be, it was an answer. i could live with that.
however, my faith in God was severely shaken. my
confusion about "God's will" was great. why was it
He seemed to make will and me feel so differently
about this? tears would cloud my eyes over and
over.

a week later, i called kirk.

"can you stop by and see me at my office?"

"sure...."

"kirk, i am mourning. i need closure to this baby.
can you tell me about the family who took her? i
mean...are they kind and loving? was it a good
home?"

"an amazing story, ann. these people adopted a
black baby three years ago, and had been praying
for two years for a sibling with some black blood.
it was a miracle to them. tremendous,
salt-of-the-earth people. it is a perfect situation."

a quietness enfolded me. i loved the story. it
brought so much order to my confusion. God knew

all along the right home for that baby, but He allowed will and me to be a part of the bigger picture so we could grow. could learn to relate better to each other. could develop new intimacies in our relationship. new freedoms.

i understood. *that* home was where the baby belonged. with a big, three-year-old brother. God does work through submission. i can trust Him in will's life. i do not have to control. His way is perfect. paul billheimer says, "the stress of marriage and the home are designed to produce brokenness, to wean one from self-centeredness, and to produce the graces of sacrificial love and gentleness."

taking the most exquisite little italian knit bunting from the chest, and wrapping it, i gave it to kirk.

"could you deliver this to that family? for the baby. they do not need to know who sent it. just that someone celebrates."

> "in His time…in His time…He makes all things beautiful…in His time. Lord, please show me every day, as i go along the way, that you do just what you say…in Your time."

a week later, i was hospitalized for seven days from a serious reaction to the fertility drugs. how could i have cared for a newborn? God, through will, took care of me.

back to normal. that is what we were trying to achieve. the adoption issue resolved. peace and quiet. it was a few days past my period, but i was sure the trauma had created that. when it was seven days past, my doctor suggested i go have a blood test. my dreams had been so dashed over the little adoptive baby, and i had had enough negative pregnancy tests to know HOW devastating that is. there was a part of me that could not bear one more blow. yet, the hope, regardless of how earnestly i was trying to push it down, returned. it looked pretty optimistic. oh, i wanted this gift to my life so much.

the lab, after drawing my blood, told me to call around 5:00 p.m. for the results.

the closer the clock turned toward five, the more shaken i became. something deep within me said the results would be negative. i became so troubled that i called jan in cleveland.

"honey, i am so scared. there is no way i can call the lab and receive a negative report. would you call for me, long distance? i would rather hear the answer from you."

a few minutes later, i grabbed the receiver as the phone rang. it would be jan. my heart was in my throat. my mouth dry. "ann...."

it was just the way she said my name. i already

knew the answer. "it was negative...."

some guttural, buried pain came screaming out
from me. the intensity greater than anything i had
ever known before.

"no, jan," wrenching sobs pouring out of me.

"no..." i screamed. i hung up. the convulsive,
mournful cries nearly took my breath away.
stumbling into the bedroom, i threw myself across
the floor, facedown. at this point, my fragility
nearly took me over the brink. there was no
reserve of courage left.

"God, where are you? You do not love me. You do
not even seem to know i am dying. jan is pregnant
again, and she did not even have to try. oh, Jesus,
the darkness is sucking me under. i have tried, but
how strong do you think i am...?"

the lines of some song i had heard began forming
in my mind. something about all of life
disintegrating, but 'praise the Lord...Jesus comes to
those who praise Him...praise the Lord....'' i tried
to do that. over and over.

the agony exceeded every other dark time. it was
the climactic, final blow to the last two years.
suddenly, i knew there was no deeper to go. too
many funerals. too many hopes dashed and buried.
when one gets to a certain level of pain, it becomes

apparent that the human soul can take no more. the world might still come crashing down around me, but something had died in me, and death would guard me from any more lethal doses of agony.

everything about me became subdued. dull. numb. removed. for the first time in my life, my confidence in God was ready to topple. i did not know who God was, or who i was, or why i should ever again believe for happy tomorrows.

here is a piece of a letter i wrote to armand, who is my friend. "dear armand, i have been too lost...in too much pain...paralyzed...numb.

"when i have gone through my *most difficult* places in life, there has always been something positive to support my weak ego strengths. something to shadow the hell. to tone it down. soften it. but the last two years, one thing after another has been peeled away from my life. EVERYTHING that was a part of my security...my coverup...and i have stood, naked and stripped, before God, myself, the world. the sense of self-hate, of inferiority, of lostness, of humiliation, of despair has wrenched the DEEPEST parts of me. uprooted and torn away the ENTIRE foundation i have existed on. and left me shaking. at times, seething. screaming. dying, and yet living. TOTALLY lost. TOTALLY without hope. TOTALLY without self-value. self-esteem.

"I love will very much. he is brilliant and strong and agressive and tremendously creative. but we need to share on a deeper level.

"i have moved to a community full of loving, kind people, but have been unable to find my place. my identity. my mission. my speaking trips, the trek around the world, all the escapades to jackson hole and sun valley…they were thrilling, BUT THEN i came HOME…to the real world, the day-in-and-day-out…and the pain was unbearable. i have never been very good at intimacy. it is one thing to be "intimate" on some level with the world, but another thing altogether in a one-on-one encounter.

"i am TERRIFIED. i do not feel good enough. i do not feel i have ANYTHING to offer, especially when you strip away boston and gym children and lots of friends in the neighborhood and good works and marathons. AND, worst of all, when you uncover the most feared defect of all: my inability so far to deliver a baby into this world.

"then, there has been my sickness. i value wellness SO, and i have never been so UNWELL. i have been hospitalized eight times since i married."

once again, the divine call

about a week later, after will was sound asleep...i
slipped out of bed to the living room. having come
to the conclusion that God could not love me, i
began to question everything. joy and peace had
long been lost in me. burying my face in my lap, i
began quietly, fervently, to go over all my years.
childhood. hawaii. college. i could see, in my mind,
how God had been my dearest Companion.
Confidant. HE had given me jan. had ALWAYS
brought a sunrise after drenching rain. He had
covered my whole life with such love and
goodness. such compassion. suddenly, i saw it
clearly: He DOES love me. He ALWAYS has. why
should He stop now?

He has been tearing down the entire foundation i
have built on to teach me about grace. grace for the
ugly feelings about my body...my lack of worth

and goodness. i am a newborn at this experience, but it washed over and over me as i sat in a heap on the couch.

peace and joy returned. silent tears. thanksgiving hope. i told Jesus that EVERY TIME i surrendered about my baby, the unbelievable gnawing and hunger for one would rise again, and my pain returned.

but…in that silent, dark living room on an ordinary night, i REALLY DID want His grace and a sense of self-love more than anything external. all these years i had been trying to find and hold on to all the external gifts, thinking they would bring the healing.

how often i have heard others say, like me, "if only i were married…or had a child…or my husband had a more substantial job…or my mother did not live down the street…IF ONLY…." how human it is to want God, but not God exclusively. we long for God WITH all the externals added on.

now i understood. ANY gift…be it a child…or whatever…will never bring the wholeness, the joy.

if He did not want me to have a child, if He had something else for me, I KNEW He would take the hunger away. this was not a pleading or a threat. it was a KNOWING. a calm assurance i could trust. watchman nee says we can never learn anything new about God except through adversity. it was all i have tried to share that led me to know the touch of God...letting Him break us thoroughly enough that He can reach down and find and touch the wounded part. THAT is all anyone ever needs to be victorious.

joyce landorf, my very dear friend, wrote me recently, "ann, the things which have shattered me the most have really stripped away the spirit of spiritual pride and given, in its place, a sense of reality theology. i am on more honest terms with God and myself than i have EVER been."

a new way of "seeing"

for weeks, i did not see how i could write this
book. all the tears. the vulnerability. telling you,
my friends, things i have never shared with
anyone. things i did not fully understand until
recently.

in my thinking, it seemed the book should end
with some incredible news like...i am PREGNANT.
after all, i had always believed it was the external
accomplishments that would make you love me.
but now i understood. the greatest blessing, bar
none, in life, is being touched in some deep way by
Jesus. carrying the Gift inside. one ALWAYS laughs
again after the valley.

in my last book, you read about julie, will's sister,
who really was the one who nagged will and
prayed for four years that he would meet me. i

told you that her husband, tom, had tried for
eleven years to be accepted into medical school.
that tom had received so many rejections. still
believed. continued doing graduate studies.

a physician happened to read I GAVE GOD TIME,
and was so moved by tom's courage and
determination, that he went to work on his behalf.
today, tom is in medical school in kansas city. julie
is getting her master's in psychology. Jesus pays.
they gave God time, and the dream is alive. a
reality. prayerfully, someday, far away from most
of the world, in a rural community in america, tom
and julie want to bring healing, through Christ, to
their corner.

i had also told about pete and mary ellen stewart.
how he started college as a probationary student.
they had three children. he worked almost full
time to support the family, and went to school in
between. they had never purchased anything
except a rocking chair for nursing the babies, and a
mattress. they rarely ate out. mary ellen cooked
EVERYTHING from scratch. they maintained a
large garden. peter rebuilt old cars for their
transportation.

"ann, when i learned to yield to God's right to do
whatever He desired to me and to my children,
then He set me free emotionally to express the
whole gamut of my feelings to Him. the psalms
became a great source of comfort and

encouragement. i could identify with the open, honest agony, and despair and confusion, and i did experience the uplifting of my soul. and i knew God would give me the grace and strength each day to keep on being responsible where i was because i knew i was in His will..." shared mary ellen.

"when times of discouragement came (usually when we had come to the point of having no money) we would begin to think we had misread God's leading and were on the wrong course. then, something would happen to start us once again on toward the next semester's classes."

peter graduated in may '82, magna cum laude, being voted the outstanding geology student of the year by his professors. but the recession had hit the mining industry hard. graduating geology students for two years had not been able to find permanent employment. in the end, they were sending resumes as far away as england and saudi arabia.

miraculously, after all the years of struggle...all the hours mary ellen was raising three little boys, and peter was working and studying...all the sacrifices...God opened a permanent job for peter right in boise, where they lived.

"even Jesus was perfected through suffering, ann" said mary ellen. "peter and i have the assurance that God is building our character."

i have been happy and contented in a different
way ever since that silent, dark night i spent with
God. idaho falls looks different to me. and the
people. it is the perfect place in the world for will
and me right now. there is a new meaning. i began
to love others in a fresh, much more relaxed way.
will, and not babies, became my priority. for the
first time, i REALLY began to enjoy him. to feel
complete, with just the two of us.

anwar sadat said, "suffering crystallizes the
soul...."
solzhenitsyn said, "prison, i love you. you have
been good to me."
bonhoeffer seemed to have a finer grasp of grace
than any other theologian i had read.

anne morrow lindbergh once said,
"pain does not make you great. if it did, the whole
world would be great...
because everyone has suffered." but....

it is how you open your life to pain. what you let
Jesus do with it. it is becoming friends, and
walking beside it, in peace and not resistance. j. r.
miller says, "we do not know how much we owe
to suffering. many of the richest blessings that
have come down to us from the past are the fruit
of sorrow and pain."

on one occasion my parents were visiting. we wish they could come more often, but my dad is always preaching, almost EVERY sunday, SOMEWHERE in the northern california area.

the little nursery door was closed.
i was in the kitchen preparing dinner.
my mom said, "honey, can i go into the little room and look around?"

"sure, mummy," i said with a smile.
I wanted to go with her, but my hands were covered with flour and pie crust dough.

a while later she came into the kitchen, audibly sobbing. we threw our arms around each other.

"oh, mummy, do not cry. it is all right. i am not sad anymore. i KNOW God will give us a baby. in His time. i KNOW."

"yes...." my mother stopped to wipe her face with some kleenex. "i was in there, looking at all the little things, and i just began weeping. i could not bear for you to hurt so. to have gone through so much suffering. but the Lord seemed to say, 'praise ME...praise ME....My way is better. something good is going to happen.... and i stood there, honey, and started praising God. i KNOW it is going to be ok."

i love you, mummy.

when i was small,
you were always so positive and happy and bright
and optimistic.
even when daddy was sick with the flu and said
he might be dying.
or one of us was disobedient. or God led daddy to a
new pastorate,
with an old, drab parsonage.
we have cried together a lot this year.
you and i. in hospital rooms. over phone calls.
in my deepest heart,
i want to be a mother like you.
and bake homemade, warm cakes late at night.
and help make airplane models.
dress paper dolls.
always smell good and look wonderful and have
style and
stand beside will as you always have by daddy.
you are my ideal.

will hears my first speech

will did not hear me give a real speech until seven
days after we were married. i was contracted to
speak at a small town in canada to address a large
group of canadian women, coming in from one
whole province. will, sitting on the first row of
this darkened auditorium, knew everyone in the
room was watching him. he told me later it was
very difficult to stay awake during my simple little
stories of cabdrivers and dreams and chocolate chip
cookies. he was so much more academic about his
faith. he liked being intellectually stimulated.

he heard a lady sniffle behind him. "oh, brother,"
he thought, "there are probably colds all over the
place, and ann and i will get sick on our
honeymoon."

a lady next to him blew her nose. and another one

across the aisle. he was sure many of them had
come from farther north where it was colder. there
was no hope for us to escape this epidemic. tired
and uneasy, he became more and more restless.

suddenly, his senses were acute. startled, he
realized these women were crying. all over the
auditorium he could hear them. it was not colds,
but touched hearts.

"ann, i felt the hair rise on the back of my neck. i
sat up straight. immediately, i was tuned in to
every word you were saying. i felt like the
centurion at the foot of the Cross. a spectator. a
disinterested party. as he watched the events, he
exclaimed, 'this surely is the Son of God.' ann, i
realized it was not what you were saying, but that
the Holy Spirit was touching people as you shared
your life, and people were being profoundly
changed.

"ann...God has His hand on you. someday He
might choose to lay this ministry on someone else.
it is truly a gift."

i could hardly wait for june 7, 1982, to arrive.
married one whole year. i would have made it.
been more of a veteran. for months, people had
said, "how long have you been married?"

we told them.

"oh, you are newlyweds. you are just getting started."

besides, my dear friend armand told me the first year of marriage is often the most difficult. so many transitions and adjustments.

it was easier after the first year. i did relax some. there was still a big part of me, though, that wanted to help will change. one of my greatest struggles was his insatiable hunger for books. or magazines. or newspapers. he LOVED to read!

my struggle with will's books

sitting at breakfast. and dinner. a book under his
nose. always, if the television was on, an open book
in his hand so he would not miss either one.
walking through airports, rushing to our gates, he
longingly looks everywhere for a deserted
newspaper under some chair. boarding a plane,
finding me a blanket. rushing to the magazine slots
and returning to his seat with four or five. usually
science or business oriented. he starts at the front
and reads straight through. one almost senses he
will be disappointed if the plane lands before he
collects all the data and files it away in his brain.

there is always a book in the car. will would not
want to be deserted anywhere without one.

i always thought i was an avid reader, but i noticed
myself backing away. what i should have done was

join him, but i was so afraid we would both become book fanatics, and completely remove ourselves from the world around us. often, i have run out to the idling car to find will sitting behind the wheel, glued to a book. in moments, i have said, "will, either that book stays home or i do. i will NOT compete with the book!" he never did well, as none of us does, with ultimatums.

there is a very positive side to this. we can sit down across from ANYONE...any occupation...and will can relate to that person about sports, world news...computers...agriculture...wall street. he hands out computerized brain information i have never heard about. what a gift his love for books will be for our children. what a brilliant overview of the world they will gain. i think i will send him in and have him read his books aloud to each child...to help them all grow up as smart as their daddy.

will's and my interests are so different in reading. i want people books. how they feel. where they hurt and struggle. their dreams. i have noticed that, more and more, will keeps picking up my books and getting into them. finally, i made him promise NOT to touch my books until i am finished with them. chuck colson is the only one who has solved the problem for us. he gave us two copies of his magnificent latest book, LOVING GOD. we each had one.

television is a diversion for will after an intense, long day. i am usually cleaning up the kitchen or baking something. our tastes in tv are opposite, too. he loves mystery and science fiction and john wayne and political debates. i am always wanting to see barbara walters' specials or some program on the educational channel about dying. we have a remote control for our television, and often, just as i am becoming absorbed in a special on handicapped children or such, he will flip the channel.

"will…!"

"honey, why do you always want to watch all the sad and heartbreaking stories?"

"because that is life…."

the ranch

on will's ranch is a large potato-packing plant. one
walks in and is amazed by the moving belts and
thousands of bolts and gadgets and noise and
activity. on the second level, overlooking the entire
plant, are offices.

for several years, will has leased the plant to other
farmers. when he decided to open it and run it
himself for two or three weeks during the
summer, he was amazed by the
grease-and-smoke-stained walls and dirt. i so
wanted to help him. to have a part in this project.
his enthusiasm about being back was contagious.
he and his dad had put this million-dollar plant
together…created some of the machinery…and
knew its inner workings better than anyone.

it was overwhelming to me to see how hard

everyone worked under this noisy, screeching roof. ever since i married will, people had told me, "your husband is the HARDEST worker i have ever known."

well, i thought he had worked hard, but so had i. they said it with such emphasis, i was always surprised. not until i saw him running the plant did i understand.

he left the house before six every morning to stop by the office, spend a while on the computer, and head on to the ranch, fifty miles away. once he arrived, he never stopped. always, energy pulsating through him. not once did i hear him raise his voice. he was aggressive and assertive and no-nonsense, but he ran around for hours helping one man in the processing area and another unloading the trucks. one day, i watched him crawl under…way down under…this massive piece of machinery to black, murky water, a welder's hat on his head. sparks began flying. at moments, i could hardly see him. it looked as if this monstrous machinery over his head was going to swallow him. i was frightened. he would help load hundred-pound bags onto trucks and crawl between what looked like life-threatening machines with a screwdriver and wrench.

always, i got up at 4:40 or 5:00 a.m., with him, to fix a big breakfast, knowing that even though i packed a lunch every day, he usually would not stop five minutes to eat it. steak and eggs. waffles and hot biscuits and pancakes and oatmeal. at least i sent him out the door with something to help carry him.

the crew were people from several places. happy to find jobs. some of them looked almost dangerous to me, but they all seemed to be earnest, hard workers. teenagers and women stood over the moving belts, sorting potatoes for hours. an arduous job. it reminded me of my days in college at birdseye, with the wet spinach. i was sympathetic and admiring of their work.

first, i hired a painter...a college girl home for the summer...to repaint all the offices in white. pam scouted carpet places for me, and i selected some sturdy, attractive carpet and had it laid wall to wall. every day, i would drive out with my container of window cleaner and ajax and paper towels and gloves and clean anything from the windows to the drinking fountain.

the women's bathroom was a disaster. out of use for several years, the toilets were black. dirt and paper were everywhere. i watched carefully everything i drank, not wanting to use the facility downstairs any more than i had to. it came to me that to be a true servant, i should clean that women's rest room for all the ladies working the lines.

it is one thing to clean your own toilets, but i never had a very strong stomach and my father ALWAYS warned me of all the germs in the public bathrooms. i prayed for courage and attacked the job with ferocious spirit, hoping that would carry me to the finish without weakening.

the stainless-steel sinks came first. they were safest. then the mirrors and floor. there was only one light close to the five toilet stalls. the others were burned out (i made a note to buy more bulbs). it was dark and eerie. cautiously, i looked around. what if a rattlesnake was curled in one of the stalls? or some ugly, nasty spider? whispering prayers, and now and then talking aloud to God, i pulled on my rubber gloves, took the sponge, and started in. i always held my breath at the most awful places, not because there was any odor. i just somehow assumed it would protect me from life-killing germs. when i finally walked away, seemingly unscathed, everything looked shining and magnificent. the men's restroom was next door, and i was sure it was at least as awful as the women's. but i had to have a break. trudging upstairs, i said to ken, one of will's men, "i came to clean the men's bathroom ...."

"ann, i will not let you even go into that place. i and some of the others will take care of it. it is not fit for a woman's eyes."

it took no effort to talk me into that offer. for days,

i would say to will as we lay between clean sheets in a clean house: "honey, pray for me. i keep seeing those awful toilets. i cannot get them out of my mind."

we would laugh and laugh. in time, i recovered. but in every hotel or airport rest room where i see a lady cleaning, i thank her. i value her in a new way.

the fifty-plus workers who were on the august run put in long hours of strenuous work. i knew will expected a lot out of them because he expected so much out of himself. it occurred to me that i could bring some surprise treats out for their three o'clock break.

one day, pam, my secretary, and i walked in with boxes and boxes of marie callendar pies from an idaho falls restaurant. when will rang the bell, and announced pie was being served, they were almost exultant. many of them had worked loyally for will over the years, and i knew they probably needed some special affirmation.

another time, it was mcdonald's milk shakes. or a big ice chest of cold drinks. everyone was always friendly and verbally grateful. it meant a great deal because i knew they all viewed me as a fragile, city lady away from her familiar elements. deeply, in me, i wanted to love them. to care. to make it easier. more than anything, i wanted to be will's helpmeet and fill in the empty places.

now, though it is winter, will is still running the packing plant and putting potatoes through for other farmers. he leaves in the dark. i stand at the window and pray until i can no longer see the pickup's lights. pray for his safety and dependence on God's wisdom. it is dark when he returns.

every morning, i ask him what he wants me to pray for.

"honey, i have not been kind lately. it really bothers me. i am under a lot of pressure, become very impatient, and start reacting in the wrong way to my people. pray for me."

"for forklift…" or "…the process grade…." most of the time, i do not have any idea what he is talking about, but i pray hourly and in moments through the day.

the phone rang one afternoon at home. "honey, there is a young guy working for me at the ranch whose girl friend is coming in from colorado for the holidays. she is attending a Bible college there and likes your books. could we have this couple over for dinner?"

knowing will's erratic, long hours at the packing plant, i hesitated.

"well…sure…but could you be home in time? what time were you thinking of?"

it was the week before Christmas. my parents were flying in from san francisco, but the only night we had available was wednesday, when they arrived.

a large roast was in the oven. with vegetables. yeast rolls. mashed potatoes and gravy. homemade pie. i had even fixed eggnog with peppermint ice cream in the blender, a frothy, predinner drink. i had met dick once or twice before, but basically i did not know either one. will had called at six. "honey, i am trying to get away in a few minutes…." obviously, he would be late, but we could wait.

finally, at 8:00 p.m., i decided we must eat. at 8:30 p.m. i served dessert. will walked in with several layers of parkas on, a billed cap with ear flaps pulled way down on his head, and his flashing smile. the guests were just getting ready to leave. my parents and i had done our best with the conversation. darling young couple.

they ended up staying while will ate. we prayed together and will called out good-night as he slipped to the bedroom after an eighteen-hour day.

in my first year of marriage, i would have been almost hysterically angry if will had invited his friends for dinner, and not shown up for the party. or been very late. now i have mellowed. i understand better the phenomenal pressure he operates under. the hours of long work. i have a better feeling for his heart, his dreams, his earnest hopes. that is helping me not to react. but there is so much give and take in a relationship like ours. i am trying ALWAYS to believe the best.

the blessing that maketh rich

my father and mother called one day and
wondered if there were any houses on the ranch
where they could come for a couple of weeks. my
dad felt he wanted to come and just walk the fields
for those days, and pray over the crops. we were
his children. this was our life. believing that
NOTHING can so effect change as prayer, they
wanted to come.

there are nine houses on the ranch. quite nice ones.
we have all-wool, wall-to-wall carpeting. modern
kitchens and baths. some houses with as many as
four bedrooms. large fireplaces. and one did
happen to be empty.

pam and i went out one morning, with will's
secretary covering our phones. with soap and
sponges and bags of groceries, we were going to

make this house a home of beauty and warmth for
my parents. pam took the bathroom. i started in
the kitchen. for hours, we scoured and scrubbed
and vacuumed and shook dead spiders out of the
draperies. the ranch is forty miles away, but we
made several trips back to idaho falls because we
kept thinking of things my parents might like. i
brought pictures off my own walls. and glenn
jenkins left one of his beautiful, large plants. a little
television. a bright, little throw rug for the
bathroom. we were EXHAUSTED when we finally
stumbled home.

but the windows shone.
and the neighbors brought in lovely furniture.
all their own idea.
it WAS quite charming.

my parents were elated. they expected outdoor
bathrooms and linoleum floors and maybe only a
little hot plate burner instead of a full kitchen. they
both grew up in kansas, and the smell of alfalfa
and the miles and miles of enormous sky and
cultivated fields and jutting mountains around the
edges...they were captivated!

every day, my father...and sometimes, my
mother...would set out across the fields. for several
days i went with my dad. the sun bearing down.
hot. dry air. slight breeze. big machinery moving
up and down the rows. giant sprinkler systems
that one could see for miles. and he would pray,

often aloud. and sing and plead with God to make this earth fertile and productive.

to use these miles of acres to feed the hungry and clothe the poor. that Jesus would be lifted up. that love would move among all the farmers and run down the roads and across the country, bringing fresh hope and strength.

hours and hours, each day,
all those in the houses…and the farmers…
could see a rather fragile man of seventy-five years,
wisps of gray hair blowing in the wind.
and they knew it was harold kiemel,
will's father-in-law,
praying over all the hopes and dreams that had
been planted in all the rows.

one of will's farmers at the ranch, vernon, was saying, "you know, there was just nothing we could do wrong this year. except for watering between the rains, we didn't have to worry."

it was the ranch's highest grain yield in history; one of the best for alfalfa; and they received more money, per sack, for potatoes than ever in the history of idaho.

will was mentioning this to ron, another one of his men.

"don't forget," ron responded, "we had ann's

140

father praying every day out there. that did
something. do you think we could get him back
next year?"

about all my father does is pray and preach and
read. as a child i remember him walking back and
forth every night, in the living room or bedroom,
praying for his children. now, i go home and he
and my mom still get on their knees every
morning, and cry and pray over every single
family member, and then the world. daddy has
made me believe that nothing great…truly
life-changing…can ever happen without prayer.

sometimes now i drive out to the ranch with will.
miles and miles spread over two sides of the
highway that he and his dad spent hours and years
clearing sagebrush from and cultivating.

i will always know, if my dad does not make it
back, that Jesus has been there. he has walked the
fields there. beside my dad. God's arm probably
wrapped around my father's aging shoulders. the
cross is planted there. high and lifted up. out
somewhere among the potatoes and grain.

will's father's dream,
and will's,
and now my dad's…
have blended
and the heart of God is leading
them toward some glorious, bright place.

sundays, our toughest days

sundays seem to be our toughest days. almost as if the enemy knows it is the sabbath, a day for worship, and he does his best to interrupt it. driving to church…or home…will and i often have intense arguments.

"honey, let's invite someone from church home with us for dinner."

"ok, let's decide who when we get there…."

in the middle of the service, often will would lean over and suggest people who were not even CLOSE to the ones i was considering. we sometimes got upset right in the middle of the church service (even though no one else knew) over who would come for sunday dinner.

one sunday morning, will said, "honey, let's see how long we can go without saying one unkind word to each other."

it sounded terrific to me, and i prayed i could keep my end of the agreement. it was an exceptional sunday. clear sky and sunshine on the windows and a gracious service and new people to greet. we came home by ourselves, after stopping at wendy's for their baked potatoes. about 4:00 p.m. i decided that, though i never did housework on sunday, after spilling cereal on the kitchen floor, i needed to haul out the vacuum cleaner, quickly. when i finished the kitchen floor, i noticed places in the dining room that needed vacuuming. we have wall-to-wall white carpet throughout the house and threads, lint, etc., show up easily. i headed for the master bedroom where will was reading and watching tv and started to plug in the vacuum.

"ANN...you are NOT going to vacuum in here.... it is sunday...come join me...."

"please, honey, it will take only a minute. i know it is noisy and creates fuzz on the screen, but i will feel so much better, since i have the vacuum out, if i quickly go over things."

will stormed passed me and headed for the guest bedroom with his book, closing the door firmly behind him. i was demolished. our pledge to each other was blotted out. here we were, upset. when i went in to talk to him, he began to tell me his reaction must go back to when he was a boy. he and his dad would be watching television and his mother would be pushing the noisy vacuum cleaner around the house. the racket, he said, was awful, and they never could see the screen very well with all the added fuzz and jerks on the screen. will's mother taught school, and the only time she had to vacuum was in the evenings. that made so much sense to me.

KNOWING why he reacted so helped me, and i regretted, anyway, making such a big deal about it. that evening, will brought in our lovely, fragrant, tall Christmas tree, and i realized the vacuum cleaner would have to come out tomorrow, anyway. there were needles from the tree everywhere. i promised myself never to do vacuuming again while will was home.

a time for reflection

so many things shaped my first two years of marriage. boston to idaho falls, idaho. total independence to submission under an authoritarian, strong man. rigid discipline in my running, to eventually no running after my pregnancy problems. tightly organized structure, to not having to get up until 10:00 a.m. if i did not want to. lots of children i was very close to, and some of my dearest friends, and a neighborhood who called me by name almost everywhere i went in boston. to a small community where i basically knew no one. i now had no specific mission in anyone's life except will's (and he was almost always reading or working or talking on the phone). i did have an office downtown, and a full-time secretary, but she handled most of the work. i would go in mostly to work on mail, a couple of days a week.

before i married, i spoke ten or twelve times a
month. now i was trying to keep it back to four or
five so as not to be away from will too much.
always, i had believed that no matter how many
books i write, or whatever large number of people
i address, if i am not real and loving and faithful in
my own neighborhood, with my husband, my life
is garbage.

never before had i broken into tears so easily, but i
found myself crying all the time. i was so lost. so
naked. so stripped. and overnight! there was not
anyone i could feel comfortable going to, to pour
my heart out to. frankly, i was awfully shy. i was
trying to bare my heart to will, but neither of us
was too adept at intimacy. sexually, we had a
beautiful relationship. but sharing our most
vulnerable parts and being tuned in to each other's
deep feelings and thoughts were things we needed
to learn.

will would often pull me down into his arms.
"honey, why are you crying so much? so many
people love you."
"i know…but i do not love me. i do not even know
who i am anymore.
i am completely lost."

on top of everything, i felt my "celebrity" status
stood out so much stronger in a small community,
where word spreads very fast, and any extra
excitement is relished. i knew how human i was.

how imperfect. how could i EVER measure up to the level of expectation around me?

my greatest blow was in not being able to get pregnant. more than not having a baby was the flaw it showed in terms of performance. all my life i set goals, and had attained them. speech contests and running marathons and getting people not to reject me. this was the first major goal i had ever longed desperately to reach, and not been able to...no matter how hard i tried. believe me. if anyone ever worked, scientifically, at making something happen, i did.

a doctor was quoted as saying "infertility patients are surpassed only by terminal cancer patients in their willingness to undergo medical procedures." i was part of that statistic. self-induced rejection, because i could not conceive, riddled me day and night.

first-love

hours, every day, i begged God to show me why i
hurt so deeply. i understood that part of it was all
the transition, but the pain was so intense i began
to realize that what i KNEW about were only
symptoms. that somewhere under the deep layers
was the root cause.

one day, God seemed to say to me, "ann, remember
all the people you have tried to love in My name?
all the speaking, writing, running achievements?
all the love and energy you have poured out to
others? do you recall what you felt deep inside, as a
child in hawaii? all the subtle rejection? i know you
love Me, but the main motivation all these years
was to be so loving, so smart, so kind, so successful
that no one would ever reject you again. out of
fear, you have unconsciously loved yourself more
than ME, and that will always keep you from

wholeness. I must be your first love."

it was the truth. it came across the walls and tables, into my heart, and illumined dark corners i had never seen before. for years, i had built my life around false securities. things that would block out my terrible inferiority and fear of rejection way down underneath. those feelings were still very much alive, festering, while i had been building magnificent towers to hide them.

one of many of God's purposes, i am sure, in my marrying will anderson and moving to idaho away from the familiar and dear, was to create in me wholeness. it has not been an easy task, i am sure, for God, and it definitely has been a "trial by fire" for me.

"i would have you learn when temptations assail you, and the 'enemy comes in like a flood' that this thing is from ME, that your weakness needs MY might, and your safety lies in letting ME fight for you" (paul billheimer, DON'T WASTE YOUR SORROWS).

perfection had been my goal as far back as i could remember. our holiness church emphasized "be ye perfect, as i am perfect." my father prayed every day, over and over, that God would wash away "every atom of sin and self." he and my mother seemed so perfect. if he prayed for that, how far away from that hope i was.

besides, if somehow i could become perfect, then i would always be loved, and never ignored. when i was little, i was always trying to achieve this. crawling out of bed, in the quiet dark, i would find a pencil and paper, and write little poems by flashlight. when i heard a girl prodigy pianist, close to my age, play some magnificent debussy piece, i would go to the piano for hours and hours, trying to make it happen for me. in the classroom, when the teacher asked a question, i waved my hand in the air. most of the time i thought i knew the answer. once in a while, i raised my hand with an animated look on my face because i wanted her to *think* i knew.

i hated weakness. it could never bring you into good standing with the world or God. the main person, my entire life, who has kept me from feeling too weak, is my twin sister, jan. she was my number one supporter. she thought there was nothing i could not do. my main motivation to excel was to keep reinforcing in her mind this truth. after all, having one person whom you love believe so absolutely in your GOOD is all one really needs to march into the world and achieve something great.

when we were in first grade, i suggested to a little girl that she and i each draw a picture, and jan would decide which one was best. that seemed a very safe risk to me. when we took our pictures to jan, she pointed to the other girl's picture, all the while whispering, "i really like yours better. i just did not want to hurt her feelings." whether that was true or not, it was all i needed. who cared what the other girl thought? i had not failed to prove i was a very good, worthy leader for jan to follow.

i remember the first day of school each year through the upper grades. it was my most dreaded experience. watching jan, with her skinny white legs and curly hair and sweet face, made me know EXACTLY what i looked like. a mirror cannot come close to showing that kind of reality. and it was so easy to see the flaws instead of the good things. jan, of course, had the same picture in her mind, through me. and we were entering a world of lovely, olive faces and shiny, black hair and dark eyes. probably, a hawaiian child would feel equally inferior in a world of creamy, fair complexions. i would walk into the classroom, terrified by the thought that other children would look at me, knowing i stood out so obviously. our minority status was so apparent. at recess, all the kids had groups and games and i desperately tried to look occupied so no one would feel sorry for me. recess and lunch were my most hated hours every day. even through high school. jan, my only confidante, was always in different classes and groups. we had the same i.q., but my parents decided we should be individuals, which was very wise.

my parents were not athletically inclined. my

father always walked several miles a day, and my mother swam now and then. but we children were never encouraged on an individual level. my brother, fred, played basketball and football, but it was not something we talked about over dinner, or went to the games to cheer. as a result, jan and i felt we were athletic morons. another blow to our bodies. we often came in from school, and took naps because we did not know what else to do. or fixed butter and sugar on bread and ate it. i'm glad we had fast metabolisms.

when teams chose up during p.e., i was often one of the last to be picked. i cried inside every time the teacher announced we were going to have relays or softball, and assigned two girls to start picking whomever they wanted. i despised p.e. every year because i felt so helpless in it. no one had ever taken time to teach me how to catch or hit a ball. my coordination was very average because it was never stretched...tested...refined. looking back, jan and i had tall, lithe bodies, and we probably could have done fairly well. deciding for the very first time to start running at thirty-four years of age, and running six 26.4-mile marathons my first year, revealed some innate capability. ONLY when i started running did i begin to feel good about my body. i was not a klutz. i could stand next to the rest of the world and feel relatively at par with them. no wonder running captivated me, and then nearly destroyed me when i was given the option of babies or running. an impossible position for me.

when i started running, i had a funny gait. leaned
too far forward, arms rigid. a girl who had been a
five- or six-miler for years, hooked up with me in
boston. i would meet her at 5:30 or 6:00 a.m. in the
dark and ice and snow, and we would run
together. i dreaded the mornings when joan was to
meet me. she was so fast, and not wanting her to
forsake me, i nearly killed myself more than once
trying to keep up. she would stop after five miles
or so, and i would fall back into an easier stride.
she told me, after i had run several marathons,
"ann, when i first ran with you, you looked
terrible. you were slow, and your form was bad. in
my mind, i would say, 'she is never going to
qualify for boston. she will never make it. she may
have a skinny body, but she is not a runner.' "

in time, my running became very smooth and
relaxed. now and then i challenged joan to keep up
with me. but deciding to do such an athletic feat
was a momentous decision. i had a thirty-four-year
handicap behind me.

running did something for me that nothing else
ever has. jan, nor will. nor best-selling books nor
full auditoriums. not getting straight A's now and
then. for the most part, i feel safe socially and
intellectually, and even spiritually. but i feel my
body is my real defective place. the more i ran, the

more whole i felt. my body was experiencing some of its potential.

jan and i dressed alike until college. every morning, we would go to our closet and agree on what we should wear. our self-esteem was already low, and we carefully tried to decide what outfit would most enhance us. some mornings we each wanted to wear something different. my mother would come in and say, "why don't you each wear what you want? you do not have to dress alike."

to us, there was no option. the only recognition outside our home, as it was, was our twinhood.

"oh, look...twins."

"aren't they cute...dressed exactly alike."

it did, also, serve as our detriment, in that we were never viewed as individuals. as two. people almost always related to us as one identity. often, different ones would come and peer into our faces, about an inch away, trying to find any freckle or turn of the nose that would identify who was who. we hated that, already feeling homely. what if they found some flaw we were trying to hide? more rejection.

we always walked out the door dressed exactly alike. until college. there might have been some tears and fussing, but we were NOT going to relinquish the only tool we had to be affirmed.

even if it meant we had no separate identity, at least we were recognized.

jan and i craved the attention of our older brother, fred. in our childish thinking, he was the hero. however, we were born in a time when few multiple births took place. my father was pastoring a rather large church where no minister in years had had babies. at five and a half, fred lost most of his out-of-the-family affirmation to everyone's enthusiasm over us. big brothers are not great fans of little sisters anyway, but fred basically ignored us. he never spoke to us, unless he was upset. at mealtimes or in the car or sitting around the house, he acted as if we did not exist. that form of rejection…complete indifference…lasted over the years until we were out of college and in our later twenties.

today, fred and i are very close. our whole family loves his wife marlene, and we adore their daughter tasha, and little son sean paul. still, the early wound to jan and me was deep, and reinforced our bad feelings about ourselves.

there must have been immense guilt hidden in me somewhere. when i was eight or nine, i would suddenly stop, wherever i was, fall on my knees, clench my hands together, and pray. then get up and go on. jan would see me, or my mother, and ask what i was doing.

"i feel so terrible inside. if i do not do that, i am afraid God will not forgive me and take me to heaven."

it did not last more than a few months, but i consciously had to keep reminding myself that God really loved me and forgave me when i asked Him, without requiring me to go through this little charade.

i love the nazarene church. my father has been a minister in it for fifty-five years. it has provided him his livelihood, clothed and fed us, and taught us God's love. today, i can sing almost any hymn in the book, all four or five verses. one of jan's and my favorite games, as children, was to pretend we were the visiting evangelist and musician. pulling out my mother's high heels, we would go to the sanctuary and, for hours, preach and sing and give invitations to people to come to the altar. then we'd cry and pray loudly over the seeking souls.

my entire social context came from the church. it was our world. sunday morning and evening, wednesday nights. daily, servicemen or troubled couples coming by the house for counseling. eating in our parishioners' homes and helping my mother with vacation Bible school and Easter/Christmas programs.

the most significant tenet in the nazarene church is its standard of holiness. on total and throughout-life surrender to the will of God. they call it sanctification in our church. it had the most profound effect on my spiritual discernment. today, i long for holiness as a bird longs for air in which to fly. my exertion of faith was built around works, not grace. i never internalized grace, only guilt.

i long for grace greater than my sin. grace that totally values my personhood in the eyes of God. grace that says, "you are human and imperfect, but i made you exactly as i wanted you...and you are beautiful." grace that washes away the pain from a truly penitent heart, so i do not have to recall over and over how weak and bad, at times, i have been.

if i heard of ANY contest that was even close to being within the realm of my accomplishment, i entered. forensics. student body offices. commencement speeches. though always frightened, i craved reassurance of my value. no matter how much i trembled, walking into strange classrooms on unknown campuses, finding students giving oratory or oral presentations, i would go and give the speech my best. then i would be sick with dread when the results were posted and i checked to see if my name was listed. sometimes it was; other times, it was not. i never gave up.

when i graduated from college, i remember saying to myself, "this is a sad moment. i will miss so much in life now. never again can i stand and speak because there are no speech tournaments out in the real world." i had received some recognition through that, and knew i would have to try something else now. it NEVER occurred to me that i would write books and lecture.

there were people who, along the way, made me feel i had real potential; others leaving vivid memories of rejection. once, in college, someone came up to me and said, "i do not like you. i do not hate you. i feel nothing for you." that was the epitome of being nothingness in someone's eyes.

throughout my grade school and high school years, there was never a teacher that made a profound impact on me. and never can i remember being in strong conflict with any of them. of course, i worked so diligently to do my best and stay out of the way, i can understand that. but not once did a teacher make me feel i was a beautiful creation with something to offer the world. until college.

it was in my parents' hearts that jan and i attend a nazarene liberal arts college. my father relinquished his beloved pastorate in hawaii, and took us all to nampa, idaho, where there was not only a nazarene college, but a church that invited dad to pastor.

miss wilson, almost as broad as she was tall, was the journalism teacher, advisor to the school paper and other related activities. no one on campus was more admired and respected than she. always a twinkle in her eyes, her tight curly hair neatly in place, she had a contagious enthusiasm. i made only Bs from her in my freshman writing class, but she took a unique interest in me.

"ann, will you do some features for the newspaper? i have an idea for a feature on dr. _____ . could you do that for me?"

if there were any publicity pictures she needed for the school or city papers, she would use me and ask my advice and suggest i run for some particular office. i probably never would have had the courage to write a book without miss wilson's early nurturing.

to hawaii, and my father's church, there once

moved a prominent businessman and his family, the homer powells. they had a daughter, sandee, one year younger than jan and i, and we were fast friends. and are to this day. one evening, homer asked my mother about our dress sizes. we had so admired a lovely "squaw" dress he had bought sandee, never imagining we could each have one. one sunday, he and his wife arrived with two large boxes. and enclosed were two turquoise and silver and white squaw dresses. probably the first "bought" dresses we had ever had. my mother is a superb seamstress, and would copy designer dresses for us, but in our minds they still did not have the magic of store dresses. it was the most glamorous thing we could think of.

"mrs. kiemel, you have two of the nicest girls i have ever known," homer once told my mother.

as jan says, we played that record over and over in our minds, for years. "very nice girls." it was the single most important piece of information about ourselves that we had ever received outside our home.

behind every encounter was my desperate need to be liked. from my earliest recollections of childhood, i had gathered all the negative data about myself. the freckles on my shoulders from the sun. my white, blah skin (which would have been normal in other states). my great fear of being seen in a swimsuit because i looked so sickly to all the brown bodies around me.

today, i realize there is almost no verbal affirmation passed from one person to the next. we all think nice things about people, but rarely do we make the effort to express them. because almost never did people outside my home praise me for anything (one lady exclaimed as jan and i ran to kiss my mother good-night, "oh, what BIG feet they have!") i came into adulthood without the adequate nutrients of value. today, if i EVER see a family at another table in a restaurant, warmly interacting…or a well-dressed man in the elevator…or notice something pretty about a lady or little girl…i stop and say what i feel. it takes such little effort and time, and over and over i watch the magic spread across their faces.

jan and i always made good grades in school without having to study too arduously. we tried to be friendly. to smile. to fit in. but being foreigners…outsiders…noticed only, really, by the color of our eyes and skin, convinced us it was because of how we looked that we were left out. in almost everything else, we excelled.

through the years, God's love has smoothed a clear path for me. He has brought many people along to love me and reassure me. He has given me some unusual successes because He knew, i guess, how much i needed them to hold on to. but way down in the gut of me, somewhere, i have always failed to understand where true worth comes from. i have failed to like me. to accept the flaws, knowing God allowed them for my development and His destiny for me in the world.

never do i take a compliment lightly. anything kind or thoughtful said to me is something i treasure. every friendship i value far more significantly than i otherwise would have. i know its worth, because i have been in the excruciating place of feeling completely alone. if i had not had God's gift of jan, i do not think i would have made it. it is very easy to understand how fred must have struggled. he had no one. romans 8:28 is the powerful beauty behind all this. God can take ANYTHING and work it for our good.

in the VELVETEEN RABBIT, there is a conversation between the rabbit and the skin horse:

> "what is REAL?" asked the rabbit one day, when they were lying side by side near the nursery fender, before nana came to tidy the room. "does it mean having things that buzz inside you and a stick-out handle?"

> "real is not how you are made," said the skin horse. "it's a thing that happens to you. when a child loves you for a long, long time, not just to play with, but REALLY loves you, then you become real."

> "does it hurt?" asked the rabbit.

"sometimes," said the skin horse, for he was always truthful.

"when you are real you do not mind being hurt."

"does it happen all at once, like being wound up," he asked, "or bit by bit?"

"it does not happen all at once," said the skin horse, "you become. it takes a long time. that is why it does not often happen to people who break easily, or have sharp edges, or have to be carefully kept. generally, by the time you are real, most of your hair has been loved off, and your eyes drop out and you get loose in the joints and very shabby. but things do not matter at all, because once you are real, you cannot be ugly. except to people who do not understand."

a new opportunity

"is ann in?" asked a warm, energetic male voice on the other end of the telephone.

"no," responded my secretary. "can i help you?"

"this is bill armstrong from colorado. i am in pocatello [fifty miles from idaho falls] and would like to drive over and have lunch with ann."

"are you the senator?" pam asked.

"yes."

years before, i had met bill armstrong and his wife ellen, when dr. bill bright brought me to arrowhead springs to address an executive conference. the armstrongs were in the audience. i chatted with them afterward, and was strangely warmed and touched by the quality of life they both exuded. we had not connected for years, and when pam called me at home, i was delighted. she called pocatello and arranged for lunch.

bill armstrong had his exceptionally lovely daughter anne, with him. his first question was, "how do you like idaho?"

quietly it began to pour out of me. my two–and–a–half years of struggle through the transition. all the positives i had discovered about a small community, but the inability to find my place here. my pleading with God to bring me a mission. a dream for this new corner. i talked about will. how worth it to have waited thirty-five years. how exciting he was to live with. but no babies. never before having lived in a small community. missing the children of boston, and all my projects with them.

"bill, i have cried. i have sat in our house and read for hours. i have buried my face in our quilt on the bed and literally thought for long stretches of time about what i might be able to do here. one morning, i told will i was not coming home until, that very day, i had found God's mission for me in idaho falls. there were visits to the volunteer corrections board. to the foster family services....

"bill, all my life, Jesus has given me my jobs. my work. will says He has put me on the shelf for a couple of years because i was exhausted…had been on a fast track for too long…and needed to rest. to renew. it has been so difficult. i am not used to months of rest and renewal."

he listened intently, as did anne. i was as vulnerable as i knew how to be. suddenly i realized i had not asked him the BIG question in my mind.

"what are YOU doing in idaho?"

he proceeded to tell me how he and ellen had wanted to buy a television station for some time, and had finally chosen the ABC affiliate, channel 6, in pocatello. that he had a fine partner, brian hogan, who would be around most of the time because, of course, his hours were spent in washington, d.c. they had decided not to turn the station into an all-Christian broadcast, nor go cable…but leave it as it is, and quietly bring in more quality and spiritual programming.

"ann, when our mutual friend, ron jensen, told me you and your husband were in idaho, i was elated. ellen and i want you to do whatever you want on the air. secular. religious. interviews. news commentaries. you choose what is comfortable for you."

this would be brand–new for me. i had done a lot of television, but had always been the interviewee.

167

now the role would be reversed. and God was
giving me all of southeast idaho to touch in His
name.

brian, bill's partner, IS terrific. the crew friendly. i
am a baby, still drinking milk, but they are patient
and enthusiastic. they are giving me creative
opportunities to share God's love…and human
struggles…and dreams that can live in everyday
people because of an extraordinary God. they have
handed me a tool to touch my world in a way i
never could before.

i am so small.
so everyday.
so simple.
i am a little scared.
the mission is big, and i am just david,
the shepherd boy.

it was not like anything i had imagined or prayed
for.
but so much better.
just like will, my husband.
just like all my life with Jesus.

God, i have always loved YOUR ideas.
they are so much finer than mine.
thanks, God, for my new mission.
make me creative, give me ideas.

for the old man in his rocker.

the young mother ironing.
the child. teenager. father.

take me, via television, and put sunshine
on the walls. and love between the doors.
and tenderness around the pain.

lonely people, crying.
take my one simple life,
and make them laugh again....

our first vacation together

someday, jan and i knew we would be "ladies" with husbands and have babies and go on vacations together. it sounded so romantic and perfect.

after being married for two years, will and i were on our way to mexico city for me to address an international youth convention for the nazarene church. will suggested tom and jan meet us there, and after my appearance, the four of us go to an exotic vacation spot in mexico for ten days. everything fell into place, and it would be mild merely to say jan and i were excited.

it was hot and sultry when we arrived in mexico city about 5:10 p.m. my hair was instantly limp, my skin sticky, and i knew NO spanish. will is secure and easy to travel the world with. he

gone…and i longed for the teens to take my place in reminding the world that Jesus lives.

i called will to the stage, spontaneously, and he told how years ago, as a new believer, he had come with a university group to mexico to sell Bibles, and a nazarene mexican minister had let him and the others sleep in his little church. the crowd loved will. he is dynamic onstage, even if he says, "this is not my thing, ann…." the experience years before changed will's life—he will never forget. after the meeting, a mexican man quietly slipped through the crowd to will. it was the same mexican minister. will threw his arms around him. they both cried for joy.

tom and jan (three months pregnant) arrived in mexico city, and i ran through all the crowds, past the guards, past security, to throw my arms around them. will preferred staying with our bags where one was supposed to be. all the way to the next stop, jan and i hung on to each other. talked a hundred words a minute. were inseparable. fortunately, our husbands enjoy each other immensely, and are not threatened by jan's and my intense closeness and love.

will had so built up this resort (though he had never been to this particular one), that we KNEW we were headed for paradise. though this was a new spot for him, how could the brochures steer us too far off course? i had traveled the world for years, speaking, but all i ever saw was the airport, then my hotel, the auditorium, and the city flashing by from a car window as i headed back to the airport. will was amazed that i could have traveled so much and seen and experienced so little.

my first clue that this exotic place might be different from what we had in mind was watching the two scantily clad, brown-bodied girls obtaining "information" on our arrival. while jan and i stood aside, they looked "wooingly" at tom and will...asked if they were married. oh, and had they brought their wives along? i was not worried about our good-looking husbands. it was these flirtatious, sensual women roaming everywhere whom i did not trust.

this particular place was buried down among rugged terrain and mountains, on the ocean. it was completely self-contained and secluded. one did not stroll down the streets looking at shops, or rent a car to go somewhere else for a day. all meals were eaten there. all sports conceivable were provided. all entertainment. very quickly we learned this was a prime vacation spot for singles. a place where the young and searching could have their human appetites totally filled. we had paid all our money up front, which was their policy. either we had to find our own game plan or lose hundreds of dollars and a vacation.

the first afternoon, jan and i were lying on the beach, soaking in some sun while the men were off playing bacci. over a loudspeaker was announced a contest of building sand castles along the shoreline, and everyone was encouraged to participate. it had been years since i had seen so many barely covering bikinis on women AND men. we had only just arrived. our skin was white. immediately, i felt again like i had as a child in hawaii. the minority. the ugly vs. the beautiful. the glamorous vs. the homely. i WAS a woman now, and married to a very exciting man, and jan and i had had years of working through some of our deep insecurities. we did know that in a few days we could be brown, too. that helped a little. but only a little.

jan and i wandered down to where at least a hundred and fifty bronzed bodies were engrossed in their works of sand art. we were shocked. there were no sand castles to be found. what they were creating i cannot mention. you may let your imagination run wild. we were DEFINITELY in for trouble. we needed about twenty vibrant Christian missionaries with us to try to redeem this heathen element.

some evenings, after our ten–or twelve–course meal (the food DID exceed our expectations), will would be the first to walk out on the entertainment. the four of us would end up in one of our two rooms, and have heavy discussions about Jesus and life and faithfulness and a lost world. sometimes, jan and i would cry. it just made our childhood memories too painful. even there people would call out, "oh, there are the twins...." we had lost our individuality all over again. we were back to being sweet, cute, nice twins.

one night, we were in tom and jan's room, and as jan excused herself, and walked into the bathroom, she let out a bloodcurdling scream. tom and will flew into the bathroom to find jan crying. "i just saw this ugly, awful cockroach. every day, i have prayed we would not have cockroaches in our room, and now i will be terrified. this whole idea was a mistake."

tom quickly stuffed paper in a little hole, and promised jan that would keep the cockroaches out. will gave his noble speech about killing lions and bears and cobras, but seeing to it that i would take care of the little creatures NO ONE should fear. was i ever fortunate to have jan there. the ten-year psychologist with her own thriving practice. the analyst who was going to find out WHY will anderson had to MAKE me lose all my fears.

"will, you cannot MAKE someone conquer her fears. you can help her understand them better, and be kind and patient, but you cannot force ann never to be afraid of anything again. that is cruel."

"well," will responded, "the BIBLE says we are not to be afraid of anything. for me, it is a mindset. a mental deciding. besides, i do not want our kids to be scared sissies."

tom had lived with a "kiemel" longer than will had, and he brought great insight and balance. every night, while all the other tourists were doing their thing, the four of us were snuggled in the plain little room, solving major issues of the world, such as cockroaches and fears and marriage.

tom is strikingly handsome. he tans beautifully just walking down the street. he was raised in florida, and loves swimming. he, like will, is a real sportsman, but had had so little time with jan lately, he chose to spend most of his hours lying in the sun...swimming...with her.

will was participating in tennis tournaments before breakfast...competing in ping-pong championships (he won)...was ALWAYS begging me to take a special snorkeling class, or a three-day scuba course. he would crawl into a small, one-man sailboat, and sail out beyond the huge boulders jutting out of the ocean, where no one was to go. lying in the sun was the LAST thing that appealed to him.

i was caught in the middle. too much sun and i was afraid of a bad burn and freckles like i got when i was a child. water sports were not what i wanted, either. swimming, though i could do it, had never been "my thing." basically, i was afraid of going six feet under the ocean, with waves crashing against rocks. learning to breathe through a tube. i did some running, but the fact that it was ninety-eight degrees every day, with just as much humidity, and all hills, took care of that. tom was getting dark and gorgeous, and will was white all over except for his face and arms. he was gone all the time except for meals. jan was becoming browner and more beautiful. will kept coaxing me to do the sports with him, but i resisted.

one afternoon, i was in our room, crying. jan

knocked, came in, surprised to see my tears. she had been crying two doors down, in their room.

"will is the best-known man here," she said. "he is the athletic hero. tom says he is exhausted from the pressures of big business, and would rather just swim and sun. i feel will is not even part of us." tears streaming down jan's face.

"i am crying, jan, because will is so white...so busy with all the sports...and tom is getting browner, and so striking. i wish will was not so caught up in sports and would get some COLOR."

after all, as children, one of the few values we understood was having "color" like everyone else.

"jan, besides...i am stuck in between. i am such a nobody. a nothing person. i do not have nearly as much color as you. i am insecure around water sports. i just do not know what to do here. you are pregnant. you have a thriving practice in cleveland. i am living in idaho without a mission, without a baby. my old friends thousands of miles away. trying to be a perfect wife and failing all the time."

one day, i was standing at the balcony by our room. we all had to climb over a hundred steps to our rooms, which were built into the mountainsides around the water. (no wonder we could eat almost anything, and not gain weight.) i was looking down along the beach, trying to spot

jan and tom and will. suddenly, among the dozens
of bikini-clad girls and sailboats, i saw will. he was
surrounded by these darling girls, who, i found out
from him later, were on his sailboat team. they had
just won the big race. THAT was the moment my
attitude changed. i WAS going to like water sports,
at least while we were on vacation. i had to save
my husband.

knowing will as i do, it probably is true that he
hardly noticed all the exotic bodies. he only wanted
to WIN the athletic events. NONETHELESS, i let
him take me snorkeling where only angels would
be brave enough to go. angels and will anderson. i
sat in on his scuba diving classes. the four of us had
our own little contests in the sailboats. we went
horseback riding.

once, this girl with glitter all over her body walked
up to will as we were going in to dinner, and
patted his arm. quietly smiling, but with daggers
in my eyes, i said, "hello, i am ann. will's wife...."
and taking will's arm, my voice spilling over with
sweetness, said, "honey, let's go to dinner. i am
starving."

the four of us laughed often over that. and all of us,
even will, began counting the days before we could
leave and go to mexico city for a couple of days.
never before had i so longed for a vacation to end.
never had i been so hot and miserable when we
had put so much money into having fun. never

again would will try to persuade anyone to go to
one of these resorts.

our first vacation.
jan and i, grown women, with our husbands.
childhood dreams do not, somehow, connect with
real, grown-up
reality.
but it did teach us.
it is a memory.
we can laugh.

another baby needs a home

it was dark outside. early morning. i was getting
ready to fly to florida for an appearance. will was
taking five extra minutes in bed before getting
ready to head for the ranch. the phone rang.

"ann…this is jan…an obstetrician in the east called
and said she has a girl who is to deliver a baby in
two weeks. she wondered if you and will would be
interested in it?"

"YES!" i said, without hesitation. without asking
will.

"YES…tell her we are. that will and i will talk
about it and call for more details."

hanging up, i crawled back under the covers in the
dark, next to will. putting my face directly next to
his in the dark, i whispered, "honey, jan's
doctor-friend has a baby for us. due in two weeks.
what do you think?"

"oh, no, Lord, not this again…" was all he could groan.

i flew to florida and spoke. i stopped in baton rouge, louisiana, with my dear friends rolfe and dot mccollister, to take some days to work on this book. jan was there to help me. in the back of my mind was the pervading thought of this baby. overall, however, i tried to block it. to forget. there was no way i would EVER again subject myself to such enthusiastic hope for or such deep bonding to a baby. and have the dream dashed against a hopeless wall, and total brokenness of spirit falling down with it.

there were several things i decided:
i would throw my energies into getting this book completed.
i would stay DETACHED.
i would not come on too strong with will, and exert pressure.

then facts started coming in, through jan. the baby's parents were exceptionally bright, educated, healthy. very pretty mother. clean family history. parents with blue eyes and dark hair. a couple who was not going to marry. who wanted higher degrees in education. subtly…quietly…my heart began reaching out to this unborn child who it appeared would fit in perfectly to our home. would probably even look like us. a deep, gentle bonding began to take place in me, and NOTHING seemed

183

to be able to stop it. as earnestly as i tried to intellecualize my thinking around it...to steel my heart against any more pain...i fell, without control, helplessly in love with this new life soon to join the world.

our real contacts with the doctor came through jan. this baby would be born on the east coast. we lived in idaho. very cautiously, i would say to will, "honey, have you thought much about this baby?"

"not really. i have just been swamped with the packing plant and buying potatoes and considering a trip with some businessmen overseas."

it was now the baby's due date, and the young mother's attorney informed us that we must make a decision one way or the other so they could start processing papers. it would be a private adoption. the family was very concerned that the baby be put in an educated home with some similar values. the obstetrician was a friend of my books, and assured the family of her confidence in "the couple." my mind was made up. i wanted this little baby. besides, how often is one offered a newborn to adopt anymore? statistics and state adoptive services say it is highly unlikely.

will said, " i will tell you what my decision is tomorrow."

decision time

it was a friday.
our friends clark and anne peddicord, and their
baby seanne, from germany, were coming in for
the weekend. they had been here, in our lives, at
such strategic moments.

after a simple, home-cooked meal, we leisurely sat
around our table visiting. several times, i had said,
"honey, can we talk to clark and anne about our
situation NOW?"

will was full of questions relating to politics and
science and spiritual concepts in Germany. he and
clark were closer than most brothers, but had very
little time together.

around 10:00 p.m., we began to tell them the story
about the baby. will started with the story of the

baby we had been offered several months earlier.

after much discussion, and many refills of hansen's lemon-lime soda, will said, "i still am not open to adoption right now. i do not believe i have any prejudices against it....it is just that i always thought we would have our own first. someday, i would like to have a family of many children, some biracial. BUT ann and i still need to work on our marriage. i don't know. it does not seem right."

smiling, through tears, i cleared the table. it was after midnight. i was exhausted. i was at another dead end. one i had promised myself i would never get into again. crawling into bed, silent and removed from will, i fell asleep on a soaked pillowcase. there was nothing i understood or felt except that new place, deep inside me that over the past year, i had, at times, lost.

"Jesus, i KNOW You love me. many moments this year, for the first time in my life, i have doubted it. but You have touched me. i have found You again. You DO love me. that is all i REALLY know."

the next morning, i fixed scrambled eggs and hot biscuits, and tried to look pleasant through swollen, tired eyes. for two–and–a–half years, i had been married to will. it seemed i understood him quite well. there was absolutely NO doubt in my mind that he loved me. that he was crazy about me. that he wanted me to be happy. this was only the third time in our marriage he had ever said "no" to me. i am pretty convincing and strong, and one of the reasons i love will is that he is stronger, and in charge.

he had said "no" to my running that time i was so ill.
"no" to the little baby three months ago.
"no" now.

clark and anne were gentle. they did not take sides. they knew me mostly through my books. they had known will and his family for years. clark and will had roomed together at the university. they knew will's genius, tough, creative dad who had probably been will's strongest influence growing up. he died before i had ever met any of them.

knowing will as i did, i was convinced that billy graham or ronald reagan or even francis schaeffer would not be able to change his mind. will is a strong, independent thinker. absolutely uncompromising. that can work both ways, good and bad.

we needed to go to pocatello, where i had a routine appointment with my doctor, don dyer. clark and anne and the baby crawled into the backseat. will and i buckled up in the front seats. pocatello is fifty miles from us. i began to cry uncontrollably. i

knew we had friends in the backseat. that i was
thirty-eight and a woman. that i did not want my
face to be smeared with mascara and completely
tear-streaked at the doctor's. but nothing helped.
my body shook as i tried to keep the sobs silent. no
one said anything. i stuck a tape into our cassette
player that is one of my favorites, "in His time."

for one hour, in the car, i grieved as i had never
done before. i could actually FEEL death. feel life
slipping away from me. at times in my life, i have
shed manipulative tears. but these were from the
most authentic, deep, inner place in me. it did not
matter what clark and anne thought. how i would
look by the time we reached pocatello. the promise
of the television possibilities with channel 6. this
book. the tomorrows. it was one sorrow too many.
i could not see how i would survive it.

the tears were dried. we walked into the hospital,
will quietly holding my hand. it was my mid-cycle,
and they were going to do an ultrasound to make
sure everything in the abdominal cavity looked all
right before they gave me the shots to induce
ovulation. one other time, i had had a terrible
reaction to the fertility drugs, and this was a
precaution.

as we waited behind curtains in the emergency
room, i looked at will. "honey, how can i say 'yes'
to something i feel is not right?" he answered
gently.

my eyes would flood again, and i would wipe
them quickly, knowing the doctor would walk in
any moment.

the ultrasound was given. my right ovary was very
enlarged. there were "multiple-multiple" cysts.
absolutely no shots could be given. don dyer said if
they had not checked first, and just given me the
injections, i would have been hospitalized within
seventy-two hours, gravely ill. i knew i had not felt
very well. now i understood why. anyway, i was
relieved. ovulating and making love to try to create
a baby in the midst of all this confusion and sorrow
was the LEAST positive thing i could think of.

driving home, with all kinds of pain medication,
and instructions to go to bed, something began to
occur to me. i had ALWAYS loved the word
"impossible." always believed in dreams. THAT
THEY MUST DIE BEFORE THEY CAN LIVE. very
quietly, deep within, i began to pray this prayer:

"Jesus, only YOU can change hearts. only YOU
make a dream live. only YOU can work in will
anderson's thinking. You taught me, the last time
around, that i could trust will. could trust YOU to
work through him. Jesus, if this baby is for us,
YOU...and only You...can change his heart. i am
weak right now. awfully fragile, God. my faith is
at its all-time low. but i pull out all the resources i
have, and believe with everything in me that You
will work out the answer to this seemingly

impossible situation...HOWEVER YOU LIKE."

it was after 6:00 p.m. when we drove in to idaho
falls. though i had left a roast and vegetables
cooking, someone suggested we just stop at marie
callendar's restaurant for dinner, and i was all for
it. my dinner could wait until tomorrow. i was sick
and emotionally exhausted.

at one point, when we stopped for gas, will got out
to check the oil. "oh, ann, i so wish we could
change will's thinking," anne peddicord said.

"anne, no one but God can...."

sitting over soup and salad, just chatting about light
things, will suddenly turned to me. steady, black,
wide-set eyes. handsome, strong face.

"ann, if you do not get pregnant this month, we
will take the baby."

tears filling his eyes. the lines on his face softening.
my eyes brimming. our arms entwined. quickly,
will pulled my arms down, and straightened in his
chair. grown men do not cry. do not show emotion.
(he says he has cried more in these two–and–a–half
years than in his whole life!)

clark and anne were radiant. little seanne, our
godchild, was smiling. light was crawling across
the walls, and into my face, filling my eyes. rivers

190

and rivers of surprise and joy spilling inside.
bathing all the wounds. healing scars. bringing
music. sending that "joy in the morning" my way.

will became exultant about this baby, still unborn.
love abounded in me for this man i had ALWAYS
deeply loved, but loved now even more because he
had given me a gift that cost himself something.

> that cost him overcoming doubts about
> whether or not he could be a good father,
> without nine months to train.

> that cost him in relinquishing his own plan, and
> surrendering instead to God's program. a
> program very different than he had planned
> years before.

> that cost him in having his own way, and
> reaching out to trust some deep place in me,
> and bringing mutuality to a major,
> life-changing decision.

before we even knew whether i had ovulated, will
was saying, "we will take this baby anyway. this is
our child!"

quickly, in spirit, he became the father of this baby,
conceived and carried by others, but given to us by
a very loving God.

our hoped-for baby arrived one evening while i
was addressing a national lutheran convention in

phoenix. a little boy. over six pounds. twenty
inches long. reported by the doctor as a completely
healthy and beautiful baby.

we had a little son.
i could think of no one who would father a son
better than will.
there would be a baby in that little crib.
the chest of drawers...the little tee shirts and
nighties...
were for him.
we would be a family. a REAL family.

before the baby was twenty-four hours old, jan
drove to and was slipped into the hospital. the
nurse unwrapped the little boy. showed his perfect,
tiny fingers and toes. fine features. rosy, clear skin.
she stretched her heart around the corner, through
the door, and encompassed this small, new soul.
and welcomed him into the family.

"i will sing to my child, i will dream with my son.
i will hold him and rock him and show him my
    love.
we will laugh, we will play, we will dance through
    the day...
with a prayer in our hearts for the world God has
    made" (merilee zdenek).

we had named him taylor jenkins anderson after
dr. kenneth taylor of *The Living Bible*, who wrote
the modern translation of the Bible for his ten

children, and then the world. after glenn jenkins,
the tough, wonderful man who helps oversee the
ranch and has been will's faithful cohort for years.

there was a thirty-day waiting period before we
could pick up the baby. we dreamed about him and
wished for him. joy danced on our bed...down the
hall...and around his little nursery. waiting.

taylor jenkins anderson.
small, fine, beautiful boy.
with cousins to play with you,
and grandparents to spoil you.
a mother to rock you and wrap you in my robe
and warm you.
and pat your bottom
and sing quiet songs on long nights.
your daddy will carry you on his shoulders,
and let you ride next to him in his big pickup.
and teach you how to ski and climb mountains and
catch trout, and read classics.
your daddy will be firm with you.
he will help God make you strong and tough.
but he will let you cry, too.
and feel deeply.
taylor, our firstborn. a son.
just what your daddy always wanted.
oh, darling boy, we celebrate you.

will wrote him a short note:

Taylor!

Welcome to this world. Welcome to Idaho.
For years, I have prayed for you. You are the
answer to my prayers.
When you are grown and have a child of your
own, then you will understand
how I feel right now.

I dream of sharing the things that my father
taught me. Camping. Fishing.
The love of work. Honesty when it costs. So many
things. You are my hope
for the future.

Your name means "industrious one." I pray to God
that my example can
build that characteristic in you. I pray that God
will make you strong
inside. That you will walk with Jesus all the days
of your life.

I have never seen you, but I know you. I believe in
you. I love you.

Your father,
Will.

hope turns to disappointment

we flew east on thursday, with diaper bag stuffed
with beautiful gowns and baby oil and
hand-knitted blanket. hearts exultant. eating ice
cream and laughing through airports and an
exhilaration known only to a couple who waits so
long. who suffers much. we were to pick up taylor
the next day. after signing papers.

en route,
without our having the slightest hint,
the mother changed her mind
and decided to keep the baby.

we returned home with empty arms. crushed
hearts. the diaper bag put away. we knelt together,
by the crib that had been there for other babies,
yet still remained empty. we offered to God
another shattered dream. we still believed He

would make beauty out of ashes.

we grieved. i felt the hot, dark waters washing
over me again, leaving me gasping for strength.
reeling by the pain of another loss. a harder blow. i
would be downtown, and someone would call out,
"how's your baby?" to face the world with another
dashed hope took courage. people were
uncomfortable. not always knowing what to say.
always so kind. we forced ourselves out, coping
with each question as it came.

we were broken, but not destroyed. cast down, but
not washed away by the sadness. i suddenly found
myself more calm and peaceful than at any other
time in my life. fire and flood and storm and
despair had wiped out my dearest wishes and
dreams. the utter abandonment of self brought
freedom and security and strength i had never
experienced.

on the road, up the steep hill where you are
trudging toward that celestial city...with splinters
of dreams here and there...and pain and
struggle...do not give up.

the rebellious child. the very ill loved one. the
broken marriage. ruined business. lost or paralyzed
limbs. the empty womb. these cannot defeat you.

"do not conform yourselves to the standards of the
world, but let God transform you inwardly by a

complete change of your mind..." romans 12:2.

God's will flows from His love. ALWAYS. a love
that seeks our long-range good, not our momentary
comfort.

amy carmichael says,

> "hast thou no scar?
> no hidden scar on foot, or side, or hand?
> i hear thee sung as might in the land,
> i hear them hail thy bright ascendant star,
> hast thou no scar?
> hast thou no wound?
> yet i was wounded by the archers, spent,
> leaned Me against a tree to die;
> and rent by ravening beasts that compassed
> Me, i swooned:
> hast THOU no wound?

> no wound? no scar?
> yet, as the Master shall the servant be.
> and pierced are the feet that follow Me;
> but thine are whole. can he have followed far
> who has no wound nor scar?"

hand Jesus your wounds, your scars.
and from them, He will create your sunrises and
your dancing hearts.
and i will stand beside you,
and celebrate.

a final word to you, my friends

this is from the deepest places in me.
i sit here, even now, tears streaming.
so many times, trying to put all this down, i have
stopped and wept. it has been my most difficult
writing assignment.
a part of me hates pain. hates weakness. defies
struggle. a part of
me is ALL weakness and pain and struggle. maybe
that is how life becomes
the more one comes to terms with the realities.
with God's truth...
that His strength is made perfect in our weakness.

my nephew tre, the family's firstborn grandchild,
is now seven years old. tall and strong with wide,
huge blue eyes. jan brought tre to an indiana
convention we addressed together. a college boy
came and picked him up at the auditorium and

played with him while his mom and i spoke.

after the convention, we got in jan's car and
headed back to cleveland. suddenly, tre, coloring in
the backseat, starting crying. he could not seem to
understand why he felt so deeply. jan would say,
"tre, tell me why you are crying."

"i do not know...i just feel sad. i did not like
telling my new friend good-bye."

we stopped for dinner. were seated in a booth. our
orders taken. jan and i were exhausted after a full
day of sharing. suddenly, tre looked up, eyes
swimming with tears. "i just remembered what
my new friend said to me, mom. 'take good care of
yourself.' and, mom, he said it with such a feeling
of love." he buried his small face in her arms, the
silent tears of feeling spilling everywhere.

i have been there all my life.
deep underneath, fragile. tender. feeling.
for myself. for the whole world.
under my smiles and warmth...behind my
speeches and marathons and
marriage...lived pain and inferiority and struggle
and hurt from years back.

and pain has led me to the reality of myself.
of wholeness that must come
not from achievement and success or a baby
but from God Himself.

199

HE must be my fulfillment.

and now i believe even more fiercely in dreams.
in the loving God.
that sunrises DO come. and surprises.
gifts. the magic moments. FOR EVERYONE.
but my love for a dream must never be greater
than my
love for the Savior. must never demand its own
timing. its own course.

in a way, in the last two years, i lost so much of
what all my life i had worked desperately, with
driven spirit, to accomplish.
God took it all away, to give me something better.
abandonment of myself that has brought true
freedom and healing.

now, with glad, reckless surrender,
i have come to peace. the process of pain and
testing
has led me to a holiness i never before was empty
enough to receive.
it makes me free to love you so much better.
and myself.
and walk more patiently with God.
no questions. no clenched fist. no stubborn will.

a baby?
in His time.

God's special surprise

two months after this manuscript was sent in,
a newborn adopted baby arrived for will and
ann.

taylor jenkins anderson. may 16, 1984...11:48
p.m. eight pounds, nine ounces.
because life is a miracle
because we waited so long
because we are so overjoyed
because God did it
because you matter to us
we celebrate!

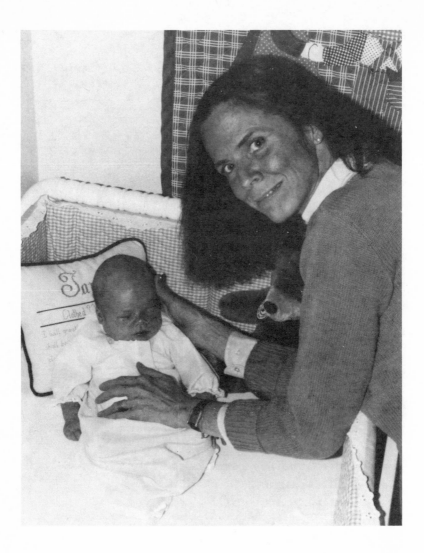

Books by Ann Kiemel Anderson

Hi! I'm Ann
I'm Out To Change My World
I Love The Word Impossible
It's Incredible!
Yes
I'm Celebrating
I'm Running to Win
I Gave God Time
Taste of Tears, Touch of God